Continuous Improvement Practice in Local Government

Local government plays a critical role in the provision of governance, infrastructure and services for local communities. Over the past 30 years, this sector has undergone significant reforms because of various superordinate governments policy changes. Continuous improvement and quality programmes have been a common tactical response undertaken by various local government organisations to remain sustainable and to continue to deliver value to their local communities. These tactical responses have had varying levels of success.

This book seeks to go beyond a tactical focus and uncover the kinds of continuous improvement practices that are enacted in various local government contexts. A focus on practices enables practitioners and researchers alike to gain insights that go beyond approaches that privilege the application of CI tools over the contextualisation of CI programs. Contextualisation affords the insightful deployment of programs that are specific to the needs and dynamics of local communities and operations.

The cases presented share insights on aspects of CI including: embedding performance measurement; harnessing learning; contextualising CI activities to support the ongoing sustainability of these practices. Researchers and practitioners alike can draw benefit from the grounded industry base experiences and insights shared in the book.

Dr Matthew Pepper is a senior lecturer within the School of Business, Faculty of Business and Law at the University of Wollongong, Australia. Research interests include operations management and continuous improvement across industry settings.

Dr Oriana Milani Price is a senior lecturer in the School of Business, Faculty of Business and Law at the University of Wollongong, Australia. Research interests include management practice, workplace learning, organisational development and change and, quality and continuous improvement, in the public sector.

Dr Arun Elias is Associate Dean (International and Accreditation) at Wellington School of Business and Government, Victoria University of Wellington, New Zealand.

Routledge Focus on Business and Management

The fields of business and management have grown exponentially as areas of research and education. This growth presents challenges for readers trying to keep up with the latest important insights. *Routledge Focus on Business and Management* presents small books on big topics and how they intersect with the world of business research.

Individually, each title in the series provides coverage of a key academic topic, whilst collectively, the series forms a comprehensive collection across the business disciplines.

Conflict, Power, and Organizational Change
Deborah A. Colwill

Human Resource Management for Organisational Change
Theoretical Formulations
Dr. Paritosh Mishra, Dr. Balvinder Shukla and Dr. R. Sujatha

Human Resource Management and the Implementation of Change
Dr. Paritosh Mishra, Dr. Balvinder Shukla and Dr. R. Sujatha

Corporate Governance Models
A Critical Assessment
Marco Mastrodascio

Continuous Improvement Practice in Local Government
Insights from Australia and New Zealand
Matthew Pepper, Oriana Price and Arun Elias

For more information about this series, please visit: www.routledge.com/Routledge-Focus-on-Business-and-Management/book-series/FBM

Continuous Improvement Practice in Local Government

Insights from Australia and New Zealand

Matthew Pepper
Oriana Milani Price and
Arun Elias

LONDON AND NEW YORK

First published 2022
by Routledge
2 Park Square, Milton Park, Abingdon, Oxon OX14 4RN

and by Routledge
605 Third Avenue, New York, NY 10158

Routledge is an imprint of the Taylor & Francis Group, an informa business

British Library Cataloguing-in-Publication Data
A catalogue record for this book is available from the British Library

Library of Congress Cataloging-in-Publication Data
Names: Pepper, Matthew, author. | Price, Oriana, author. | Elias, Arun, author.
Title: Continuous improvement practice in local government : insights from Australia and New Zealand / Matthew Pepper, Oriana Price, Arun Elias.
Description: Abingdon, Oxon ; New York, NY : Routledge, 2022. | Series: Routledge focus on business & management | Includes bibliographical references and index. |
Identifiers: LCCN 2021040962 (print) | LCCN 2021040963 (ebook) | ISBN 9780367820534 (hardback) | ISBN 9781032200347 (softcover) | ISBN 9781003011675 (ebook)
Subjects: LCSH: Local government--Australia. | Local government--New Zealand. | Continuous improvement process--Australia. | Continuous improvement process--New Zealand.
Classification: LCC JS8033 .P46 2022 (print) | LCC JS8033 (ebook) | DDC 320.8--dc23/eng/20211012
LC record available at https://lccn.loc.gov/2021040962
LC ebook record available at https://lccn.loc.gov/2021040963

ISBN: 978-0-367-82053-4 (hbk)
ISBN: 978-1-032-20034-7 (pbk)
ISBN: 978-1-003-01167-5 (ebk)

DOI: 10.4324/9781003011675

Typeset in Times
by MPS Limited, Dehradun

Contents

Figures

Tables

Acknowledgements

The authors wish to acknowledge the support and contributions of many continuous improvement practitioners and the organisations who kindly provided their time and expertise to engage, share and discuss their experiences and ideas with us throughout the process of developing this book. They include the following Councils:

City of Canterbury Bankstown Council
Blacktown City Council
Cumberland City Council
Camden Council
Kiama Municipal Council
Shellharbour City Council
Wollongong City Council
Willoughby City Council
Wollondilly Shire Council
Masterton District Council
Greater Wellington Regional Council

There are a number of people who we also worked with closely and who have been our 'critical friends'. They include Ms Simone Robards, Ms Kate Conroy and Ms Michele Piscioneri.

We also wish to acknowledge our PhD Students and Research Assistants Ms Janelle Davidson and Dr Jonathan Mackay.

Thank you to my co-authors for their support throughout this journey. To Alison, Camilla and Abigail – thank you for your love, support and patience.
MP

I thank my co-authors for being on this writing journey with me and for always finding humour. To Craig, Thomas and Lars you are always my inspiration and my cheer squad and to Laura and Franco for teaching me to believe in possibilities.
OP

Thank you to my co-authors for being part of the journey. This book is dedicated to my wife Preetha and my children Ananya and Alaap.
AE

1 Introduction

Sector overview

As a sector, local governments in Australia and New Zealand represent significant public expenditure and employment (as seen in Figure 1.1). There are 560 local governments in Australia, accounting for approximately 5% of public expenditure ($38 billion in 2018–19) and approximately 10% of national public sector employment (Commonwealth of Australia, 2017). In New Zealand, there are over 78 local government organisations that make up approximately 3.4% of public expenditure (NZ$9.7 billion in 2018), employing approximately 30,000 people (Local Councils NZ 2011). There is significant variance in how local governments operate within and between Australia and New Zealand. These differences include political oversight, governance relationships and financial resourcing. The size, geographic coverage and scope of the work of local government organisations also varies widely both within and between these two countries. Despite such differences, there is a commonality in purpose and shared aspects of historical evolution among local government organisations in both countries.

Local government plays a critical role in the provision of governance, infrastructure, and services for local communities. Governance includes local democracy via the election of local representatives and a mayor to provide input in local policy development, implementation and decision making. Infrastructure work includes the construction and maintenance of public roads and drainage, amenities, community buildings, parks and open spaces. Service may include waste management, local ordinance enforcement, development assessments and consent, public health inspections, environmental protection and community events and activities. In larger local government organisations water and sewage services may also be part of the services

DOI: 10.4324/9781003011675-1

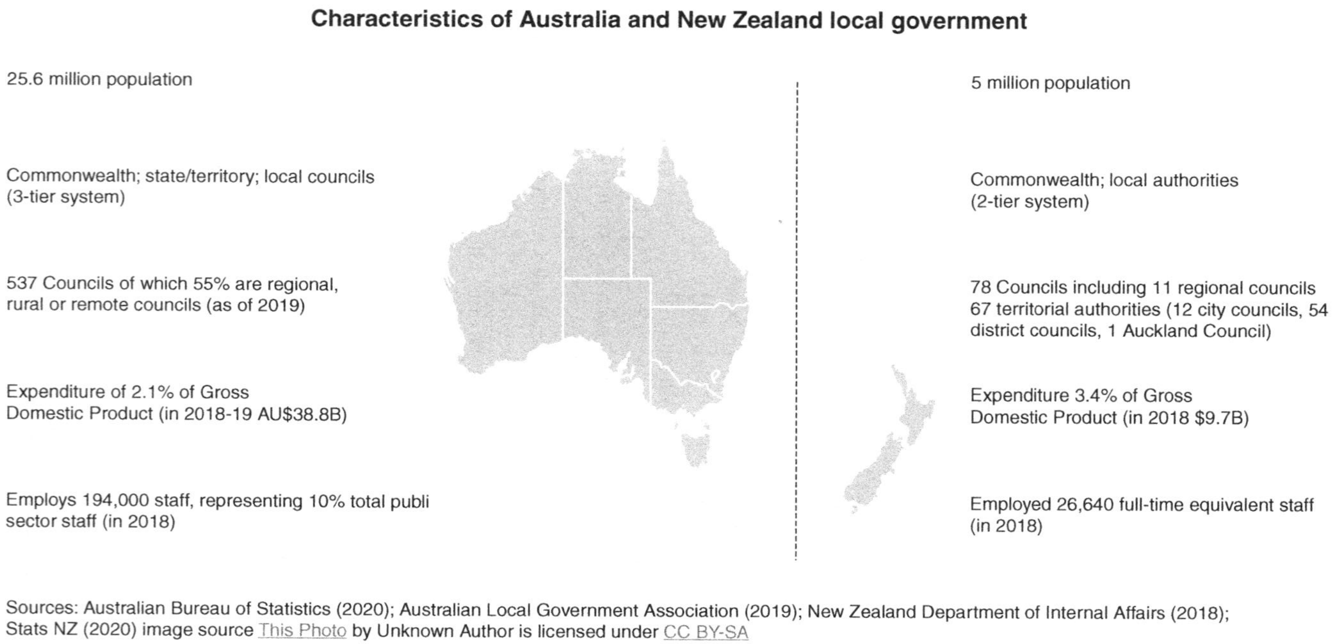

Characteristics of Australia and New Zealand local government

Australia	New Zealand
25.6 million population	5 million population
Commonwealth; state/territory; local councils (3-tier system)	Commonwealth; local authorities (2-tier system)
537 Councils of which 55% are regional, rural or remote councils (as of 2019)	78 Councils including 11 regional councils 67 territorial authorities (12 city councils, 54 district councils, 1 Auckland Council)
Expenditure of 2.1% of Gross Domestic Product (in 2018-19 AU$38.8B)	Expenditure 3.4% of Gross Domestic Product (in 2018 $9.7B)
Employs 194,000 staff, representing 10% total publi sector staff (in 2018)	Employed 26,640 full-time equivalent staff (in 2018)

Sources: Australian Bureau of Statistics (2020); Australian Local Government Association (2019); New Zealand Department of Internal Affairs (2018); Stats NZ (2020) image source This Photo by Unknown Author is licensed under CC BY-SA

Figure 1.1 Characteristics of Australia and New Zealand local government adapted from the Australian Bureau of Statistics (2020), Australian Local Government Association (2019), New Zealand Department of Internal Affairs (2018), and Stats NZ (2020).

Image source. This Photo by Unknown Author is licensed under CC BY-SA.

provided. The local grass-root community emphasis is a key feature that distinguishes local government from other levels of government in both Australia and New Zealand.

Over the past three decades, local councils have adapted operational models in response to various programs initiated by state governments in Australia and the federal government in New Zealand. The programs have aimed at encouraging local councils to become more accountable to their local communities. In recent history, these programs have included a New Public Management (NPM) agenda of reform aimed at improving efficiencies and achieving economies of scale. As early as 1984, in New Zealand, there have been examples of forced amalgamations which has resulted in the current structuring of local government into 13 regional councils and 74 territorial authorities. Though occurring later, similar but not as extensive reforms also occurred in Australia as recently as 2015. These forced amalgamations aimed at a reduction of about 25% of underperforming councils local government as part of the 'Fit For the Future Initiative' (see for example Glanville and Stuart, 2017).

In this context of change, continuous improvement (CI) and quality management (QM) programs have been a constant feature in the local government landscape. Both CI and QM in various forms (e.g., ABEF, NZBEF ISO9000, Lean, Six Sigma, Service Reviews, Service Quality, CouncilMARK™) continue to be understood as means of (1) providing guidance in the implementation of policy changes, (2) the achievement of strategic priorities and (3) operational improvement within local government organisations. The role of CI and QM as a response to legislative changes was recognised by researchers in Europe as early as 1999 (Donnelly, 1999). Similarly, in the Australian and New Zealand contexts, this was also reinforced by other researchers (see for example Houston & Katavic, 2006; Allen & Eppel, 2020; Alshumrani, Munir & Baird, 2018; Johnsson, et al., 2021). It is therefore timely to capture and discuss the evolution, various applications and experiences of CI and QM in the localised contexts of Australia and New Zealand. The overarching aim of the book is to discover these contextualisations of CI and QM that have occurred in practice.

Structure and flow of the book

This book seeks to contribute to current discourse about the practices of CI in local governments (LG) within Australia and New Zealand (ANZ). We consider current research in this context to draw out insights into the practices and future research in this discipline. The book brings together theoretical and practical insights drawing from extensive industry-based applied research. Several case studies are presented, reflecting on the application of various journeys in CI in the local government context to bring together the theory-practice nexus. The benefits of this book are designed for both academic and practical applications. Researchers and higher-degree students will gain value from some of the key themes within this discipline, and practitioners will be able to use this book as a tool to provide practical guidance and tools on how to navigate the implementation of CI in their organisations.

With this book, we aim to address several gaps within current publications. First, our focus on the application and practice of CI in local government in Australia and New Zealand addresses an area of work that is currently underrepresented in the research in this discipline. Second, we seek to translate theoretical concepts into approaches that can be applied in practice, thus bringing to the fore the theory-practice nexus. This is achieved using case studies to provide theoretically informed narratives of how approaches have been applied by practitioners in the implementation of CI in their organisations. We draw attention to the importance and benefits of academic-industry collaboration in the CI discipline for its sustainability.

Part one of this book introduces the context of CI in local government in Australia and New Zealand. Chapter 2 presents the current landscape of continuous improvement in the local government context in Australia and New Zealand. The chapter provides an orientation to the legislative and funding structures that both enable and constrain the service provision roles of local government in both countries. By drawing on extant literature, this chapter considers the ways in which local government has adopted QM and CI at different points in time. The chapter then proposes a multi-frame integrative approach as a way of contextualising quality and CI implementations. Chapter 3 explores the relationship between learning and CI. It identifies the ways in which learning may be used as a foundation to support the implementation of CI projects and build an organisation's capability to adapt to a changing environment.

In part two of the book, we introduce three case studies. Chapter 4 introduces the first case study which explores the application of stakeholder analysis as an approach within a local government in New Zealand. The chapter provides a brief overview of stakeholder theory and associated concepts, followed by a discussion of the four phases of a stakeholder analysis framework. The chapter illustrates how the framework is being applied in managing stakeholders of a continuous improvement project in a regional council context.

The second case study is presented in Chapter 5 and discusses the journey of an Australian local government organisation in the design, development and implementation of a performance management framework. It considers the critical relationship between strategic priorities, service delivery, operations and performance measurement. The chapter provides an approach that may be adopted in developing a strategic suite of measures to facilitate operational management, strategic prioritisation and communication of organisational performance to internal and external stakeholders.

Chapter 6 presents the third case study, an analysis of the critical success factors associated with CI implementations. Ten critical success factors are identified from an examination of the literature. These are then validated for relevance for New Zealand local government organisations by drawing on findings from research conducted with CI practitioners in this context.

Finally in Chapter 7, the fourth case study is presented. It discusses the work and challenges faced by CI practitioners in the local government context of both countries. It presents insights into the multifaced work of CI practitioners as they engage their organisations in both strategic and operational CI work. The chapter also considers the use of consultants as a part of local government CI deployments.

In part three of the book, we draw on the lessons learned from each of the four case studies and present our conclusion in Chapter 8. In this chapter, we draw on the key themes and learnings from the author's engagement with local government in both countries. Finally, the Appendix of this book provides templates and tools used in the case study work which may be adapted and adopted by practitioners and researchers for working and researching in local government.

In exploring the chapters of this book, readers may choose to focus on the case studies as guides to 'on the ground' applications of theoretical concepts, drawing on various tools to implement similar programs in their own organisations. Alternatively, for researchers, the case studies may provide some insights into the complexities of researching in the local government context and serve as a tool for future research endeavours. Readers may also choose to explore the various chapters as a way of introduction to CI work in the local government context.

Regardless of the approach adopted by readers, we hope that the key message is clear; a contextualised approach is necessary for the implementation of CI and QM. With this book, we endeavour to provide some insight on ways of contextualising proposed frameworks to an organisation's needs and culture. Contextualisation may be achieved by taking into account the nature of the services provided, community needs, fiscal constraints, organisational culture and capacity, as well as the emerging and changing legislative and policy context. Adapting a chosen framework and implementation strategy to support localised organisational conditions may be the most important decision in a sustainable CI initiative.

This book is the result of a joint international research project organised by the authors in 2018–19. This project was partly funded by financial and in-kind contributions by the Faculty of Business and Law, University of Wollongong, Australia and the Wellington School of Business and Government, Victoria University New Zealand. This book acknowledges the contributions of the local government partners who engaged in and supported this research project.

References

Allen, B. and Eppel, E. 2020. Holding on tight–NPM and the New Zealand performance improvement framework. *Australian Journal of Public Administration*, *79*(2), pp. 171–186. https://doi.org/10.1111/1467-8500.12405

Alshumrani, S., Munir, R. and Baird, K. 2018. Organisational culture and strategic change in Australian local governments. *Local Government Studies*, *44*(5), pp. 601–623. https://doi.org/10.1080/03003930.2018.1481398

Australian Bureau of Statistics 2020. National, state and territory population, available at: www.abs.gov.au/statistics/people/population/national-state-and-territory-population/latest-release (accessed 1 November 2020).

Australian Local Government Association 2019. Local government key facts and figures, available at: https://alga.asn.au/facts-and-figures (accessed 27 March 2020).

Commonwealth of Australia 2017. *Shifting the Dial 5 year Productivity Review*, Inquiry Report.

Donnelly, M. 1999. Making the difference: quality strategy in the public sector. *Managing Service Quality: An International Journal*, *9*(1), pp. 47–52.

Glanville, B. and Stuart, R. 2017. NSW council amalgamations scrapped after Government backflip. *ABC News*, 27 July.

Houston, D. and Katavic, M. 2006. Quality in a New Zealand local authority: A case study. *Total Quality Management and Business Excellence*, *17*(04), pp. 425–438. https://doi.org/10.1080/14783360500528148

Johnsson, M.C., Pepper, M., Price, O.M. and Richardson, L.P. 2021. "Measuring up": A systematic literature review of performance measurement in Australia and New Zealand local government. *Qualitative Research in Accounting & Management*, *18*(2), pp. 195–227. https://doi.org/10.1108/QRAM-11-2020-0184

Local Councils NZ 2011. About local government. http://www.localcouncils.govt.nz/lgip.nsf/wpg_URL/About-Local-Government-Index?OpenDocument#LocalCouncilsEconomicContributionToNew%20Zealand, accessed 27 March 2020).

New Zealand Department of Internal Affairs 2018. About local government, available at: www.localcouncils.govt.nz/lgip.nsf/wpg_URL/About-Local-Government-Index?OpenDocument (accessed 27 March 2020 and 2 November 2020).

Stats NZ 2020. New Zealand's population passes 5 million, available at: www.stats.govt.nz/news/new-zealands-population-passes-5-million (accessed 1 November 2020).

2 Landscape of continuous improvement in local government

Landscape of continuous improvement: Definitions and timeline

Much has been written about the foundation and evolution of CI in organisations, with its application in manufacturing. Initially emerging during the industrial revolution as a means of inspection at the end of production processes. Quality management as a precursor to CI emerged during the industrial revolution when the division of labour displaced responsibility for quality to inspections at the end of the production process. Checking the quality of the product through inspection gave rise to the first paradigm of quality labelled *Quality Inspection* (Weckenmann et al. 2015). When faulty products emerged, attention was given towards understanding why these occurred, as well as the cost and time impact of these.

This paved the way for the development of *Quality Control* practices that focused on addressing and removing the causes of poor quality to reduce error rates. Unlike *Quality Inspection* (which emphasised the identification of errors), the focus of *Quality Control* was on preventing errors from occurring in the first place (Weckenmann, 2015). To achieve prevention, organisations needed to invest in programs designed to identify, monitor and make the necessary adjustments to processes and/or inputs as a means of reducing product variation. This encompassed the work of Quality specialists such as Shewhart, Deming, Feigenbaum and (Dahlgaard-Park, Reyes & Chen, 2018).

Quality assurance (QA) was the next significant milestone that commenced in the 1960s and shaped the approach to quality for the next two decades. Initially, the focus was on the efficiency of processes to make products at lower costs and improve organisational profits. The focus on efficiency and cost was driven by growing of post-war prosperity and associated increased demand. At this stage, the focus was on

DOI: 10.4324/9781003011675-2

sales of existing products to customers, but as organisations matured, production efficiency was not the only goal. Production effectiveness became more important and began to involve customers in defining what constituted a quality product. This second phase showed a shift away from a manufacturer-centred view of quality and towards one that understood and encompassed end-consumer needs. In this phase, the focus on process was extended to understand the costs of quality (or not focusing on quality) more proactively. These understandings were captured, for example, in quality manuals. This saw the introduction of concepts and techniques associated with quality control cycles (Weckenmann, 2015; Dahlgaard-Park, Reyes & Chen, 2018).

In the 1980s, *Total Quality Management* (TQM) signposted the emergence of a more systemic view of quality and a stronger focus on CI. Much of this work in Europe and in the United States was driven by declining competitiveness against Japan's strong manufacturing sector. Initially named *Quality Management,* this approach included the introduction of quality standards (e.g. ISO9000:1987) and management systems, which paved the way for the present-day ISO9001:2015 standard series. The establishment of these international standards sought to acknowledge the importance of documenting and standardising an internationally recognised definition of quality. To demonstrate competence and compliance with these standards, accreditation was a key part of the system.

Accreditation became the mechanism for giving organisations a level of confidence that their business partners had both quality capabilities and competencies to deliver products that met the agreed standards (Weckenmann, 2015; Dahlgaard-Park, Reyes & Chen, 2018). Standards were adapted and applied across organisations in sectors beyond manufacturing for example, health care and more broadly occupational health and safety. Peak bodies that emerged at this time included the American Society for Quality (American Society for Quality, 2020) and the European Foundation for Quality Management (EFQM) (Conti, 2007) and the Australian Organisation for Quality. Common features were evident across these geographically based models.

In later years, and as an extension of a systemic view of quality, consolidation of various approaches occurred. The emphasis of the TQM phase extended beyond the traditional scope of manufacturing, thus encompassing broader aspects of organisations. Included in these broader aspects were the role of employees, leadership, customers, results, and processes as well as the interrelationships among these key elements. *Business Excellence* (BE) and associated models became the moniker of this phase. The European Foundation for Quality

(EFQM), The Australian Business Excellence Framework (ABEF) and Baldrige Excellence Framework are examples of such models (Carnerud & Bäckström, 2021; Dahlgaard-Park, Reyes & Chen, 2018; Weckenmann, 2015). The challenge with these emerging models was a tendency to mimick quality assurance checklists applied organisationally as a means of assessment of quality against a pre-set standard, rather than 'organisational models, aimed at representing the organisation's dynamics' (Conti, 2007 p. 116).

TQM in its various evolutions since the 1980s and 1990s seems to be the springboard for considering the influential nature of multiple aspects of organisations towards achieving quality. Though research specific to TQM became less popular, aspects of the Business Excellence frameworks which emerged during the TQM phase attracted much research attention, for example the research focusing on the relationship between quality and organisational culture (Carnerud & Bäckström, 2021). Following TQM, in more recent years, quality has gone through various permutations with the latest being Lean, Six-Sigma and Lean-Six Sigma. Emerging from manufacturing, these approaches have been adopted for the implementation of quality in organisations across various sectors including service environments and the public sector (Carnerud & Bäckström, 2021; Dahlgaard-Park, Reyes & Chen, 2018).

Though not always explicitly stated in the earlier evolutionary milestones of the quality journey, the drive to achieve better outcomes (i.e. produce quality products, reduce variation, implement standards) shows traces of an underlying imperative for continuous improvement. This is not only evident in the improvements that have occurred in production, product and service quality throughout the last century. This is can also be traced in the evolution of theory and research in this discipline, as well as the various iterations of quality frameworks discussed above.

In this section, we have provided an overview of the key milestones in the evolution of quality thinking. With this foundation now set, in the next section we go on to discuss the emergence of continuous improvement and the application of quality and continuous improvement in the context of local government in Australia and New Zealand.

The landscape continuous improvement local government in LG AU and ANZ

In the Australian context, there are seven local government jurisdictions, each governed by State or Territorial governments through their respective Local Government Acts. These legislations set out the roles and responsibilities of local government organisations and operational and funding structures, and accordingly, the state-based jurisdiction limits the role of the federal government. Some of the main areas of responsibility for servicing communities addressed by local governments within Australia include maintenance of local assets (e.g. roads, parks and sporting fields), waste and environmental management, town planning, health inspections and the development and management of community buildings (e.g. libraries) At the time of writing there were 569 local government organisations, servicing communities with diverse geographies, characteristics and needs (Dollery & Yamazaki, 2018).

Contrary to this, New Zealand has a two-tier government system. Accordingly, there is a more direct relationship between the national Parliament and local government. The role and responsibilities of NZ local government are enshrined in the Local Government Act 2002 (Reid, 2013). There are 78 regional, territorial and unitary Councils (collectively referred to as local governments) in New Zealand. These different types of local government organisation vary in the scope of responsibilities, for example regional councils' responsibilities include public transport, regional parks and bulk water supply, while territorial authorities provide local services including waste management, wastewater management, libraries and recreation, town planning and local regulations (Local Government in NZ). District and city councils are distinct in the sense of the size of the population that they serve.

Over the last three decades, local government organisations began to implement various changes to their operating models in response to various programs initiated by the Commonwealth and State Governments in Australia and the Federal Government in NZ. These programs have aimed at encouraging local councils to become more accountable to their local communities and achieve operational efficiency and effectiveness in response to Commonwealth and State directives.

These programs have included New Public Management (NPM) and consequently have led to marketisation, privatisation and competitive tendering of functions such as planning and performance management and organisational restructures. In the latter decades, the focus on competitive tendering was tempered through the concept of best value, which emphasised how services may be improved to deliver the best value to the community. Though not necessarily widely adopted, it reflected some shift in approaches in both the Australian and New Zealand contexts (Yetano, 2009; Bovaird Halachmi, 2001;

Lodge & Gill, 2011). The rationale behind Best Value is that recommendations may be embedded within annual planning and budgeting cycles (Yetano, 2009) as an ongoing organisational focus on deliverables to the local community. Given that the Best Value approach focuses on the revision of services, we argue that this approach was a precursor for the introduction of the Service Delivery Reviews framework in the Australian context in the second decade of the 2000s.

These changes in ideology, policies, priorities, and ways of working have and continue to be a key driver for the adoption of various quality management approaches as a set of 'mini-fads' (Houston & Katavic, 2006 p. 428). To support the required operational changes, local governments in Australia and New Zealand began to adopt various quality approaches. The approaches adopted were often those that were either well established in the private sector and/or in use in larger public sector organisations. This began in earnest in the early 1980s, during the *Total Quality Management* period discussed above. Frameworks such as ISO9000, Business Excellence, Strategic Service Reviews and more recently Lean Six Sigma are examples that have been adopted in the local government sector as part of improvement programs. Embedded in these frameworks is the assumption and expectation that improved outcomes are achieved through the application of various improvement cycles. Therefore, continuous improvement has emerged as an aspect key to the application of such frameworks.

The writings of seminal authors such as Deming and Imai whilst well known in the academic space are not widely discussed in the more recent local government approaches to CI. Nevertheless, these authors suggest that CI needs to be considered as an overarching organisational philosophy and cultural value. When understood as a philosophy it permeates every aspect of the organisation and work practice. For Deming, this means that management must *"improve constantly and forever the system of production and service"* (Principle 5 of transformation, Deming 1982 cited in Sanchez & Blanco, 2014 p. 998). Similarly, Imai (1986, XX) states that '*when applied to the workplace Kaizen means continuing improvement involving everyone—managers and workers alike*'. Although quality emerged as a focus of business (traditionally manufacturing) operations during the industrial revolution, the importance of works from authors such as Deming and later Imai is the more comprehensive and systematic approach to CI (Bhuiyan, Baghel, & Wilson, 2006).

In a review of three decades of quality and CI literature, Sanchez & Blanco (2014) identified 10 seminal definitions of CI These definitions were developed by various authors over three decades including seminal authors such Deming, Imai and more recently Chang. Despite the semantical interpretations of CI, a common genealogy is evident across several common aspects:

- CI is systematic and of a cyclical nature;
- waste reduction is a key imperative of CI;
- each iteration of a CI cycle incorporates incremental improvement;
- CI necessitates the involvement of multiple stakeholders;
- CI involves a change in existing organisational practices and routines;
- CI involves the measurement and tracking of improvements in performance outcomes.

We have purposefully not zoomed in on or identified a single 'best definition' or focused on the differences between definitions. This is because we believe that what is important is not the definition of CI itself, but how the core values of CI are adapted and adopted in contextualised practical applications as part of diverse quality frameworks. In the sections that follow, we will discuss the application of the various frameworks and their relationship with CI.

Standards in local government—ISO9000

In the 1990s and the decades following local government reforms were underpinned by neo-liberal ideologies and the agenda of New Public Management (NPM) (Pollitt, 1995; Worthington & Dollery, 2002). Neoliberalism, came in the form of a 'wave of market deregulation, privatization and welfare-state withdrawal' (Venugopal, 2015, p. 168) and the application of neoliberalism in the management of the public sector, came to be known as New Public Management (Reiter & Klenk, 2019). Several reforms occurred in the public sector in New Zealand and Australia, with such reforms in New Zealand commencing about five years earlier than Australia. In both countries, the focus on reform centred on improvement and a fundamental shift in the role of local government organisations. This shift sought to move the operating models from service provision to service purchasing. Though similar in their imperatives, each country followed different trajectories.

In New Zealand local government—which operates under a two-tier government system and is governed under the *Local Government Act, 2002* (and previous enactments) (Haidar, Reid & Spooner, 2011)—the emphasis was on establishing a competitive environment, which strongly embraced market principles, marketization and privatisation (Ha, 2002; Haidar, Reid, & Spooner, 2011). Alongside the sector restructuring and marketisation, the quality management philosophies were being discussed as "essential" (Houston & Katavic, 2006 p. 429). For example, one key quality framework adopted by New Zealand local governments was ISO 9000 (Houston & Katavic, 2006).

The approach in the Australian context was a less radical move towards privatisation and adopted a focus on improving government through various policy reforms. The National Competition Policy was one such policy reform. With the introduction of National, State and Local Government procurement practices as part of the policy change, the systemic application of quality management as a key criterion for the awarding of tenders was embraced. This was explicitly expressed for example in the Tendering Guidelines for NSW Local Government '*councils may request that a successful tenderer meet a recognised Quality Control system that requires the successful tenderer meet' (2009 p. 17)*. As with New Zealand, in Australia too the focus was on adopting ISO9000.

The adoption of standards (such as ISO9000) as a system for managing their operations (and contractors) was welcomed by some local government organisations. This is somewhat unsurprising, given that local government, in the enactment of their regulatory functions (Megarrity, 2011), apply various standards (e.g. building and development, food and health, asset management, engineering for roads and construction and environmental management etc.) (Abdulai, 2007) as part of local government organisations' day-to-day work. This aspect of State-driven policy could therefore be well accommodated by certain aspects of local government operations.

This shift had several implications for local governments with respect to the adoption of quality control systems and associated practices in both countries. The importance of quality in the procurement process became a priority like never before due to the shift in local government role from service provider to service purchaser. Those involved in managing capital programs via contractors and purchasing goods and services were required to develop the necessary understanding of such systems and the process of accreditation. These new bits of knowledge and understandings were necessary to comply with the requirements of the National Competition policy and tendering guidelines of the associated jurisdiction. Quality management systems, such as ISO900 gave some assurance that the contractors engaged to provide services would deliver promised quality to the community (Alam & Pacher, 2000).

Those local governments throughout Australia ascribing more deeply to neo-liberal ideologies (with various examples across NSW, Victoria across Tasmania) viewed the changing context as an opportunity for additional revenue generation. In these cases, the application of quality management took a different form. After making a strategic choice of pursuing profit-driven tendering (in other local government jurisdictions or for State Government projects) and restructuring the purchaser-provider' model, the pursuit of organisational accreditation to ISO 9000 became a priority. For example, in Australia Bankstown City Council and Liverpool City Council in NSW, Hobart and Sorell Councils in Tasmania and in New Zealand, Rotorua District Council (Houston & Katavic, 2006; Jones, 1999, 2002) sought out accreditation. Achieving such accreditation enabled these local government organisations to compete for these lucrative government contracts (Abdulai, 2007; Price, et al., 2018; Jones, 1999, 2002. In these organisations, ISO9000 standards were also used as a template for improving organisational process in operational areas identified as being contestable in the open market. The achievement of accreditation became a key imperative for these local government organisations and therefore provided key direction for the improvement efforts.

Continuous improvement therefore emerged from and was implemented as part of ISO9000 and for the purpose of the ongoing accreditation process. Accreditation was achieved by several local government organisations, bringing about benefits such as:

- Documentation of organisational procedures in line with international standards;
- gap analysis of organisational process performance via a systemic procedural framework;
- competitiveness in market contestable service provision;
- compliance to National and State purchasing policies;
- mechanism to assess the robustness of constructors' systems as an indicator of competence in delivering quality products (Houston & Katavic, 2006; Abdulai, 2007).

However, at the same time, several challenges were cited. These challenges included:

- Cost, time and resource commitment;
- 'off the shelf' solutions that do not consider cultural needs of the organisation;
- limited commitment by employees outside the quality team;

- overreliance on consultants thus limiting transfer of learning to in-house;
- fast timeframe for achievement of accreditation limited capacity for embedding new practices within the broader organisation;
- standards perceived as 'too mechanistic and static for services' (Abdulai, 2007, p. 353);
- Accreditations' focus on compliance rather than commitment to the principles (Houston & Katavic, 2006; Abdulai, 2007).

Though not all local government organisations have continued to maintain the purchaser-provider split, as many have moved away from competing for service delivery contracts in the open market. However, ISO management systems have been retained by some, including continued accreditation. The ISO management system continues to provide a mechanism for organisation to monitor and guide organisational processes and how these deliver improved services to the community. ISO accreditation is therefore a way of signalling to the community that quality service delivery is an important consideration for the local government organisation.

Business excellence frameworks – ABEF and NZBEF

In the Australian context business excellence has been articulated via the Australian Business Excellence Framework, whilst in New Zealand, the framework for business excellence is the New Zealand Business Excellence Foundation (NZBEF) model. These seminal frameworks have undergone various iterations since their inception to maintain relevance in the changing Australasian context (Saunders, Mann & Grigg, 2008). The use of business excellence frameworks is a key feature of the Total Quality Management (TQM) phase discussed in section 1.1 above.

The ABEF and NZBEF are approaches that exemplify a systemic view of quality whilst providing flexibility in the selection of tools and techniques for continuous improvement. Both frameworks identify seven key criteria to guide organisations towards building organisational sustainable performance and quality. It brings to the fore key areas for managing quality organisations including: leadership, strategy (or strategic planning), customer and stakeholders, process management, people (or workforce) and performance measurement and results. The application of the ADRI (Approach, Deployment, Results and Improvement) methodology embedded in the ABEF is used for the purpose of an internal 'current state' self-assessment. ADRI focuses attention to the purpose, implementation, results achieved as well as how results lead to improvement in organisational processes and programs (LGAM, 2020; Corbett, 2011; Grigg & Mann, 2008). The ADRI methodology has clear parallels with the Deming Cycle for continuous improvement.

A key benefit of applying a self-assessment is the identification of improvement opportunities which then can be prioritised and captured in an organisational wide continuous improvement program use to drive targeted improvement projects. The use of self-assessment encourages a cyclical approach to monitoring the impact of continuous improvement initiatives. The regular application of the self-assessment can be used to provide feedback on the progress of overall organisational improvement. Furthermore, as both frameworks have been adopted by multiple organisations in the local government sector in both countries, a comparison of practices between organisation is possible. This supports the sharing of 'good practices', experiences and innovation (Grigg & Mann, 2008; Saunders, Mann, & Grigg 2008; Mohammad, et al., 2011).

According to the UTS Centre for Local Government (ACELG), Australian local governments have adopted the ABEF as an umbrella system to facilitate the integration of continuous improvement imperatives within their organisations. In a survey of local governments implementing the ABEF, of the 19 local government organisations survey, more than 50% had used the framework for less than 5 years and of that number more than. 42% more than 5 years. The survey respondents also reported several benefits from applying the ABEF. These included: *"structured process for continuous improvement; better communication and shared commitment to improvements; team building and alignment to corporate priorities; financial savings; and access to best practice"* (ACELG, 2010 p. 10–12). In contrast, some of the challenges identified in the application of the ABEF included: "*resources and commitment required over time; language inappropriate to local government; overemphasis on assessment and quantifying improvement; private sector focus which excludes community and councillors; turnover in leadership which results in a lack of organisational commitment; lack of information applicable to local government*" (ACELG, 2011 p. 10–12). It is evident from the above research, while not a panacea in all situations, there is much that can be harnessed from the application of this framework to set solid foundations for CI. The identification of challenges signals ways in which those intending to adopt or continue to use the framework in their organisations can ameliorate its application.

These findings are not dissimilar to previous work by the authors of this book. In Price, et al. (2018) the ABEF was used as a guiding framework for the implementation of the continuous improvement program. In the local government organisations studied by the authors, improvement projects included those focused on strategic planning and performance measurement via the application of models such as the balanced scorecard to support improvements in the strategic and results criteria (Johnsson, et al., 2021). Therefore, the ABEF via the application of self-assessment, could be viewed as a platform for continuous improvement to address elements of the framework in which the organisation has identified as critical to achieving improved performance and strategic alignment (Price, 2000).

Another interesting finding from an industry-based survey by Artist (2010) was that in addition to the use of the ABEF or other frameworks, there were many activities which local government organisations recognised as aspects of continuous improvement. These included: collating and analysing comparative data about the performance of various programs including people engagement, risk management and service delivery reviews; working with various internal and external stakeholders, including taskforces, community and employees; developing workforce capacity through various programs including performance appraisal, feedback and development, leadership development, reward and recognition. What can be drawn from these findings is that there is considerable time and resource investment in activities which contribute to organisational improvement. However, as this finding only pertained to 50% of respondents (Artist, 2010), questions then arise as to whether the remaining 50% of respondents either did not engage in a broad range of activities that may contribute to organisational improvement or did not identify such activities as CI (Artist, 2010). It also raised further questions: if such activities were undertaken, why were they not recognised as improvement activities? Was it because they were undertaken outside of the imperatives of a formal continuous improvement framework? The findings of the latter study by ACELG (2011) which found that about 50% of respondents had adopted the ABEF for less than 5 years may suggest that such recent application of the framework perhaps plays a role in such activities not being recognised as CI. The application of the ABEF and associated self-assessment tool can be useful in the identification of such broader organisational activities as contributing to CI.

Current thinking and practice – Applications of Lean Six Sigma in local government

The beginnings and evolution of Lean and Six Sigma (LSS) are well established and documented as emerging from manufacturing (Brady & Allen, 2006. With a core philosophy of value creation and flow, driven by a deep understanding of customer needs, the focus of improvement is minimising process variation and waste. These values and foci may be one of the reasons for the transition of this approach and its application in contexts outside of manufacturing. However, through providing an attractive option for the implementation of continuous improvement for the public sector this has not come without challenges. The work of Radnor (2010) in the application of Lean in the other public sector organisations found that the central challenge stems from the contextual differences between private and public sector organisations. Specifically, differences that pertain to the nature of operations, service environment complexities and diverse customer needs and identities. These differences also relate to local government.

Characteristic of local government organisations are priorities driven by political influence, challenges in aligning diverse strategic imperatives with operational capacity under resource constraint. The cumulative impact of these factors needs to be acknowledged when considering effectiveness and resource requirements of LSS as a management framework within this context (Suarez Barraza, et al., 2009). Local government as a public service needs to articulate value across multiple services often used by the same customer. This may present a challenge in delivering such value consistently across all services. For example, the same customer may experience satisfaction in one service while at the same time be dissatisfied by the service and value provided by other services delivered by the same organisation. Therefore, in the local government sector, what constitutes value is polysemic.

Although there are challenges with the application of LSS, Antony et al. (2016) maintain that LSS can provide a mechanism to achieve a balance between competing imperatives such as service delivery for stakeholders, reductions in costs and operational efficiencies. In addition, Elias (2016) proposes that an in-depth stakeholder analysis is a good starting point for the implement of LSS in this context. The application of LSS techniques and tools in this context need to be enacted differently than in the private sector. In place of a standalone approach, LSS tends to be implemented alongside other programs. Findings from local government research in the application of LSS by Price et al. (2018) demonstrated that LSS provides a focused methodology for the implementation of continuous improvement as part of the already adopted Australian Business Excellence Framework (ABEF).

The findings from this research build on the work of Corbett (2011), who conducted a comparative investigation between NZ and US local government organisations. The organisations researched embedded LSS within already existing quality frameworks such as the Baldrige Criteria for Performance Excellence (BCPE). Corbett (2011) suggests that in combining approaches, BCPE could be used to provide an overarching structure for LSS, with LSS making a positive contribution to a culture of continuous improvement within an organisation. This is not uncommon in the local government context, where various methodologies are enacted through business excellence frameworks.

There is potential to develop what Bhuiyan & Baghel (2005) call *hybrid methodologies*. This is not a new concept. As early 2002, Boyne (2002) highlighted the synergistic relationship between TQM and the best value approach as both have a similar set of practices (e.g. continuous improvement, customer focus and teamwork). Building on this idea of overlap between approaches and frameworks, we argue that Service Delivery Reviews represent the next evolutionary step to the Best Value framework. In research conducted by Walker & Gray (2012), it was found that Service Delivery Reviews were implemented with the dual imperatives of improved financial outcomes and quality of services. This dual purpose of service reviews was in response to increasing demands for service provision in a context of reduced resourcing.

Service reviews may therefore be integrated with existing organisation quality frameworks, including LSS, to produce contextualised (hybrid) implementations. Positive synergies could also be achieved by combining LSS with the Service Delivery Reviews. According to ACELG (2012 p. 7): '*A service delivery review aims to drive more efficient use of resources whilst providing services to meet the needs of the community… a service delivery review can take a "whole of organisation" approach or just cover one department, service or strategic focus area*'. The implementation of the Strategic Service Review framework should include an analysis of service delivery processes, documenting service profiles to identify gaps in service provision quality. The advantage of linking service reviews with LSS is that the methodology and tools from LLS provide a formal improvement approach to complement the analysis steps of the Service Review framework.

State Government reforms continue to impact local government. The 'Fit for the Future' initiative in NSW and the 'Victorian Reforms program' in Victoria (NSW Government, 2014a, 2014b; Dollery & Drew, 2018) are recent examples. In research conducted by the author of this book (see, Price, et al., 2018) service reviews were used extensively in anticipation of having to demonstrate 'fitness' in terms of viable service delivery. The application of service reviews focused on both community-facing services such as leisure, community services and libraries in addition to internal-facing services such as cleaning and records management. These reviews had varying degrees of success. Although some resulted improvements in the value proposition for customers while at the same time achieving improved economic and efficiency imperatives, others did not. A key difference between those reviews that resulted in improvements and those that did not, was the level of ongoing commitment and investment in service-based continuous improvement activities. We argue that it may serve local government organisations well to link service review programs to robust methodologies such as LSS as well as the organisation's overarching improvement program.

Waypoints in the continuous improvement landscape in local government

The landscape of continuous improvement and quality in local government has mirrored that of the industry at large. In this broader context, continuous improvement and quality have evolved over several decades resulting in various frameworks and approaches all of which make a contribution and respond to the changing environmental conditions. Quality and continuous improvement were introduced in local government in Australia and New Zealand in response to various reforms principal of which was NPM. NPM was a key driver for the adoption of certain private-sector management practices and outcomes as part of a new way of conducting the 'business' of local government. In response, various continuous improvement and quality frameworks were adopted as part of the suite of new management practices to enable improved efficiency, effectiveness and the creation of value for communities.

In our view the landscape of continuous improvement and quality in local government may be characterised through several observations:

- A variety of continuous improvement approaches and frameworks have been adopted by local government organisations over the last

four decades and these have tended to follow trends that have been established in the private sector.
- Significant investments have been made and substantial experience and competencies have been developed in the implementation of these various frameworks.
- Embedding of continuous improvement as an organisational practice has not always been sustained.
- It is not uncommon for multiple frameworks and methodologies to be adopted in parallel to one another (e.g., ISO9000, business excellence frameworks, LSS and Service Delivery Reviews), resulting in hybridised approaches.
- The adoption of hybridised approaches may be a way of:
  - Responding to top-down state governments' policies.
  - Capitalising on pre-existing and embedded competencies, skills and preferences.
  - Adopting and sharing approaches (and methodologies) already successfully used by other local government organisations.
  - Managing the contextualisation of frameworks to meet the emerging needs of local government organisations and their stakeholders.

Concluding comments

There is inherent complexity in the nature of local government, complexity which is often not directly experienced in the private sector. Local government must respond to numerous changing strategic parameters (e.g. respective State Governments policy shifts and political pressures at the local level), while at the same time responding to community needs under fiscal constraints. Identifying what is valued by numerous and diverse stakeholder groups while attempting to deliver such value diversity in an efficient and effective manner is challenging. This diversity emphasises the importance of understanding stakeholders' expectations and requirements at every level of the organisation and making the creation of value a central tenet. The diversity of local government organisations means that several continuous improvement and quality approaches and frameworks can be adopted. Failing to develop hybridised approaches where the links between various models are made, reduces opportunities for contextualisation and may lead to continuous improvement being perceived as just another 'fad'.

References

Abdulai, K.M. 2007. *Municipal reforms in Tasmania: The impact of the purchaser-provider split on service delivery in Hobart and Sorell councils*, PhD dissertation, University of Tasmania.

Australian Centre of Excellence in Local Government 2010. Overview of 14 Excellence Frameworks and Tools, University of Technology, Sydney.

Alam, Q. and Pacher, J. 2000. Impact of compulsory competitive tendering on the structure and performance of local government systems in the State of Victoria. *Public Administration and Development: The International Journal of Management Research and Practice*, *20*(5), pp. 359–371. https://doi.org/10.1002/pad.146

American Society for Quality (ASQ). https://asq.org/quality-resources/iso-9000 date sourced 01 December 2020.

Antony, J., Rodgers, B. and Gijo, E.V. 2016. Can Lean Six Sigma make UK public sector organisations more efficient and effective?. *International Journal of Productivity and Performance Management*, *65*(7), pp. 995–1002. https://doi.org/10.1108/IJPPM-03-2016-0069

Artist, S. 2010. *Implementing the Australian Business Excellence framework in Australian Local Government*, University of Technology Sydney.

Bhuiyan, N., Baghel, A. and Wilson, J. 2006. A sustainable continuous improvement methodology at an aerospace company. *International Journal of Productivity and Performance Management*, *55*(8), pp. 671–687. https://doi.org/10.1108/17410400610710206

Bhuiyan, N., Baghel, A. 2005. An overview of continuous improvement: From the past to the present. *Management Decision*, *43*(5), pp. 761–771. https://doi.org/10.1108/00251740510597761

Bovaird, T. and Halachmi, A. 2001. Learning from international approaches to best value. *Policy & Politics*, *29*(4), pp. 451–463. https://doi.org/10.1332/0305573012501468

Brady, J.E. and Allen, T.T. 2006. Six Sigma literature: A review and agenda for future research. *Quality and reliability engineering International*, *22*(3), pp. 335–367. https://doi.org/10.1002/qre.769

Carnerud, D. and Bäckström, I. 2021. Four decades of research on quality: Summarising, Trendspotting and looking ahead. *Total Quality Management & Business Excellence*, *32*(9–10) pp. 1023–1045. https://doi.org/10.1080/14783363.2019.1655397

Conti, T.A. 2007. A history and review of the European Quality Award Model. *The TQM magazine*, *19*(2), pp. 112–128. https://doi.org/10.1108/09544780710729962

Corbett, L.M. 2011. Lean Six Sigma: The contribution to business excellence. *International Journal of Lean Six Sigma*, *2*(2), pp. 118–131. https://doi.org/10.1108/20401461111135019

Dahlgaard-Park, S.M., Reyes, L. and Chen, C.K. 2018. The evolution and convergence of total quality management and management theories. *Total*

Quality Management & Business Excellence, *29*(9-10), pp. 1108–1128. https://doi.org/10.1080/14783363.2018.1486556

Dollery, B.E. and Drew, J.J. 2018. Chalk and cheese: A comparative analysis of local government reform processes in New South Wales and Victoria. *International Journal of Public Administration*, *41*(11), pp. 847–858. https://doi.org/10.1080/01900692.2017.1298609

Dollery, B.E. and Yamazaki, K. 2018. Is bigger really better? A comparative analysis of municipal mergers in Australian and Japanese Local Government. *International Journal of Public Administration*, *41*(9), pp. 725–734. https://doi.org/10.1080/01900692.2017.1298127

Elias, A.A. 2016. Stakeholder analysis for Lean Six Sigma project management. *International Journal of Lean Six Sigma*, *7*(4), pp. 394–405. https://doi.org/10.1108/IJLSS-11-2015-0046

Grigg, N. and Mann, R. 2008. Review of the Australian Business Excellence Framework: A comparison of national strategies for designing, administering and promoting. Business Excellence Frameworks. *Total Quality Management & Business Excellence*, *19*(11), pp. 1173–1188. https://doi.org/10.1080/14783360802323669

Ha, Yeon-Seob. 2002. Comparative Study of Budgetary and Financial Management Reforms: The Cases of Australia, New Zealand, and Sweden. *International Review of Public Administration*, 7(1), pp. 123–136. DOI: 10.1080/12294659.2002.10804998

Haidar, A., Reid, M. and Spooner, K. 2011. Politicisation but not responsiveness: Preferences and experiences of New Zealand councillors. *Australian Journal of Political Science*, *46*(3), pp. 453–472. https://doi.org/10.1080/10361146.2011.595388

Houston, D. and Katavic, M. 2006. Quality in a New Zealand Local Authority: A case study. *Total Quality Management and Business Excellence*, *17*(4), pp. 425–438. https://doi.org/10.1080/14783360500528148

Imai, M. 1986. *KAIZEN - the Key to Japan's Competitive Success*, Random House, New York, NY.

Johnsson, M.C., Pepper, M., Price, O.M. and Richardson, L.P. 2021. "Measuring up": A systematic literature review of performance measurement in Australia and New Zealand local government. *Qualitative Research in Accounting & Management*, 18(2), pp.195-227.https://doi.org/10.1108/QRAM-11-2020-0184

Jones, R. 1999. Implementing decentralised reform in local government: Leadership lessons from the Australian experience. *International Journal of Public Sector Management*, *12*(1), pp. 63–77. https://doi.org/10.1108/09513559910262689

Jones, R. 2002. Leading change in local government: The tension between evolutionary and frame-breaking reform in NSW. *Australian Journal of Public Administration*, *61*(3), pp. 38–53. https://doi.org/10.1111/1467-8500.00283

LGAM 2020. Australian business excellence framework, http://www.lgam.info/australian-business-excellence-framework

Lodge, M. and Gill, D. 2011. Towards a new era of administrative reform? The myth of post-NPM in New Zealand. *Governance: An International Journal of Policy, Administration, and Institutions*, *24*(1), pp. 141–166. https://doi.org/10.1111/j.1468-0491.2010.01508.x

Lyndon Megarrity Politics and Public Administration Section 31 January 2011. *Local government and the Commonwealth: an evolving relationship. Research Paper no. 10 2010–11*. https://www.aph.gov.au/About_Parliament/Parliamentary_Departments/Parliamentary_Library/pubs/rp/rp1011/11RP10#_Toc284229058 (accessed 22 March 2021).

Megarrity, L. 2011. Local government and the Commonwealth: an evolving relationship. Research Paper no. 10 2010–11. https://www.aph.gov.au/About_Parliament/Parliamentary_Departments/Parliamentary_Library/pubs/rp/rp1011/11RP10#_Toc284229058

Mohammad, M., Mann, R., Grigg, N. and Wagner, J. P. 2011. Business Excellence Model: An overarching framework for managing and aligning multiple organisational improvement initiatives. *Total Quality Management & Business Excellence*, *22*(11), pp. 1213–1236. https://doi.org/10.1080/14783363.2011.624774

NSW Government 2014a. Fit For the Future – A Blueprint for the future of Local Government. http://www.fitforthefuture.nsw.gov.au/sites/fftf/files/Fit-for-the-Future-A-Blueprint-for-the-future-of-Local-Government.pdf (accessed 1 September 2015).

NSW Government 2014b. Fit for the future – A roadmap for stronger, smarter councils. http://www.fitforthefuture.nsw.gov.au/content/fit-future-roadmap-stronger-smarter-councils (accessed 1 September 2015).

Pollitt, C. 1995. Justification by works or by faith? Evaluating the new public management. *Evaluation*, *1*(2), pp. 133–154. https://doi.org/10.1177%2F135638909500100202

Price, O. 2000. The balanced scorecard at Bankstown City Council. Paper presented at the *Implementing the Balanced Scorecard in Local Government. Hilton Sydney Airport 29 August, 2000*.

Price, O.M., Pepper, M. and Stewart, M. 2018. Lean Six Sigma and the Australian business excellence framework: An exploratory case within local government. *International Journal of Lean Six Sigma*, *9*(2), pp. 185–198. https://doi.org/10.1108/IJLSS-01-2017-0010

Radnor, Z. 2010. Transferring lean into government. *Journal of Manufacturing Technology Management*, *21*(3), pp. 411–428. https://doi.org/10.1108/17410381011024368

Reid, M. 2013. Amalgamation in New Zealand: An unfinished story? *Public Finance and Management*, *13*(3), pp. 239–265.

Reiter, R. and Klenk, T. 2019. The manifold meanings of 'post-New Public Management'–A systematic literature review. *International Review of*

Administrative Sciences, *85*(1), pp. 11–27. https://doi.org/10.1177%2F0020852318759736

Sanchez, L. and Blanco, B. 2014. Three decades of continuous improvement. *Total Quality Management & Business Excellence*, *25*(9–10), pp. 986–1001. https://doi.org/10.1080/14783363.2013.856547

Saunders, M., Mann, R.S. and Grigg, N.P. 2008. Utilisation of business excellence models: Australian and international experience. *The TQM Journal*, *20*(6), pp. 651–663. https://doi.org/10.1108/17542730810909392

Suarez Barraza, M.F., Smith, T. and Mi Dahlgaard-Park, S. 2009. Lean-kaizen public service: An empirical approach in Spanish local governments. *The TQM Journal*, *21*(2), pp. 143–167. https://doi.org/10.1108/17542730910938146

Venugopal, R. 2015. Neoliberalism as concept. *Economy and Society*, *44*(2), pp. 165–187. https://doi.org/10.1080/03085147.2015.1013356

Walker G. and Gray M. 2012. *Service delivery reviews in Australian local government*. Australian Centre of Excellence for Local Government, University of Technology, Sydney, Australia.

Weckenmann, A., Akkasoglu, G. and Werner, T. (2015). Quality management - history and trends. *TQM Journal*, *27*, pp. 281–293.

Worthington, A.C. and Dollery, B.E. 2002. An analysis of recent trends in Australian local government. *International Journal of Public Sector Management*, *15*(6), pp. 496–515. https://doi.org/10.1108/09513550210439643

Yetano, A. 2009. Managing performance at local government level: The cases of the city of Brisbane and the city of Melbourne. *Australian Journal of Public Administration*, *68*, pp. 167–181.

3 Embedding CI in LG through knowledge sharing

Defining continuous improvement (CI)

In Chapter 2, we discussed the relationship between continuous improvement and various quality approaches. We identified that CI is implied, in varying degrees, in all quality approaches both as a philosophy and organisational value (Bhuiyan & Baghel, 2005), which may then be realised through various frameworks (e.g., ABEF/ISO[1], EFQM, Baldridge) and methodologies (e.g. ADRI, PDCA, DMAIC, RADAR). Multiple definitions of continuous improvement exist and are explored by various authors. Common in aspects across the definitions presented by Sanchez & Blanco (2014)[2] are: understandings of CI as cyclical in nature; organisational in scope and integrating people at all levels of the organisation including customers; a focus on eliminating waste in systems and processes; and incrementally achieving improved outcomes. In the sections that follow, we will discuss the application of the various frameworks introduced above and their relationship with CI.

Interestingly, none of the definitions presented in Sanchez & Blanco (2014) review explicitly include learning and knowledge sharing as a concept related to CI. Yet when considering research in both critical success factors (CSF) and barriers to CI implementation, learning in its various forms (e.g. training, education, knowledge sharing) is clearly an important factor. For example, Fryer Antony & Douglas (2007) maintain that training and learning are critical to success in CI implementation, while Jurburg, Viles, Tanco & Mateo (2017) and Carnerud, Jaca & Bäckström (2018) recognise that capturing and communicating knowledge generated from CI initiatives is imperative to successful CI implementations. Conversely, in the absence of meaningful effective and ongoing training and education, the inability to build a learning organization and inadequate knowledge or understanding of CI are recognised

DOI: 10.4324/9781003011675-3

as barriers (Masters, 1996; Angell & Corbett, 2009; Singh & Singh, 2015). Clearly, this reinforces the notion that learning and knowledge sharing are necessary for embedding CI. The question remains that how can these be brought together in practice?

What is the relationship between continuous improvement and learning?

Continuous improvement is a well-researched management topic, with a well-developed theoretical relationship to learning in organisations (e.g. Kovach & Fredendall, 2013, 2014, 2015; Letmathe, Schweitzer & Zielinski, 2012). Unsurprisingly, this is also recognised and reinforced in frameworks such as the ABEF/ISO, EQMF and Baldridge, where learning and development of people is a fundamental aspect to achieve business excellence. In research conducted by Woods, Tan & Ryan (2015) from the Australian Centre of Excellence for Local Government (ACELG), it is noted that continuous improvement is perceived by local government employees as a key driver for peer learning and may be harnessed as a key mechanism for embedding learning in the organisation. It is therefore acknowledged from many perspectives that learning is important. What remains elusive for organisations, is how learning may be harnessed to enable CI to make a positive impact in practice.

Taking into consideration CSFs, barriers and framework imperatives, we suggest that it is important to consider the kinds of *learning and knowledges* that are required to facilitate CI. We suggest that not only is it important to:

- Learn knowledge *about* the concepts of CI and their application (i.e. tools, frameworks and how to use these);
- learn knowledge about *how to do* CI systemically as an organisational practice (i.e. the integration of CI interventions with strategy, culture, operations);
- learn knowledge that emerges *from* CI outcomes (i.e. new bits of knowledge that have resulted from improvement initiatives).

Interestingly, the emphasis on learning and CI was well established in the *Kaizen* philosophy on quality and continuous improvement. Developed by Imai (1986), Kaizen originated in Japan and can be understood as a ‘set of guiding principles that steer improvement and learning’ (Suárez-Barraza, Ramis-Pujol & Kerbache, 2011 p. 303). In contrast to other quality approaches which focus on continuous improvement, the Kaizen philosophy focuses on using continuous improvement tools such as the PDCA cycle (plan, do, check, act) as a way to embed learning as a means of driving organisational change towards improvements (Ramírez & Álvaro, 2017). Therefore, through the practice of Kaizen 'workers' experiences, learnings, and acquired knowledge are inherited accumulatively and shared' (Nakamori, 2019 p. 273) with others as part of a collective approach learning and working.

Drawing on the principles of Kaizen and its application in Japanese companies including Toyota Motor Company, Nonaka (1991, 2007) developed a model to explain knowledge sharing in organisations. Nonaka & Takeuchi (2007 p. 164) states '[n]ew knowledge begins with the individual', therefore learning is often understood as something that individuals do (Kovach & Fredendall, 2013). Though this is important, it is insufficient for the successful implementation of CI initiatives and for the embedding of CI as an organisational practice. This is because embedding CI as a practice requires shared understanding and action among many individuals. These shared understandings include bits of knowledge about organisational structures, systems and work.

How does this shared understanding come about through sharing of knowledge? Work conducted by Nonaka and colleagues over several decades led to the development of what is known as the Organisational Knowledge Creation Theory (OKCT) (Nonaka, 1991). The Organisational Knowledge Creation Theory (OKCT) (Nonaka, 1991) presents four propositions about the concept of knowledge that need to be understood in considering and applying Nonaka's OKCT. These are:

- Individual knowledge is a validated belief through interactions in the broader environment;
- knowledge is performed as skillful action;
- knowledge has the potential to be used by people to problem solve;
- knowledge may be explicit (i.e. codifiable and documentable) and tacit (i.e. enacted in actions but difficult to describe and verbalise) (Nonaka, 1991, 2007; Nonaka & Von Krogh, 2009).

Importantly in the context of CI, OKCT proposes a powerful approach for knowledge sharing beyond the individual and provides a useful framework for considering how organisations 'create, diffuse and retain knowledge' (Linderman, 2004 p. 593) that emerges from continuous improvement. We propose that when considering CI there are three kinds of bits of knowledge that may be foregrounded:

- Knowledge *about* the concepts of CI and their application;
- knowledge about *how to do* CI systemically as an organisational practice;
- knowledge that emerges *from* CI outcomes.

The OKCT framework depicted below can facilitate sharing (and we argue learning) of all three kinds of knowledge listed above. The framework considers, in the first instance, the sharing of tacit knowledge through 'socialization'. Next, tacit knowledge is made explicit through 'externalisation' and is built upon via the process of 'combination'. Finally, explicit knowledge is made tacit via the process of 'internalisation'. The OKCT, not unlike CI, adopts the notion of a continuous cycle (and more recently in the work of Nonaka and Toyama (2015) as a spiral), in which each iteration ideally builds and improves upon the previous. The application of each stage of the OKCT and associated model is discussed in more detail below: (Figure 3.1)

Socialization (tacit to tacit) is the sharing of tacit knowledge between individuals. This kind of knowledge (tacit) is bodily, tied to the senses, movement, intuitions and unarticulated mental models and therefore difficult to communicate. For example:

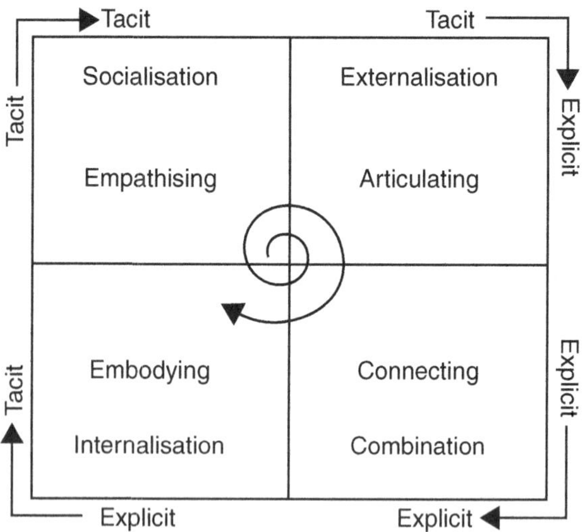

Figure 3.1 Knowledge sharing cycle.

Image source: "File:SECI model.png" by Rosanna Rossi is licensed under CC BY-SA 3.0

1. How experienced drivers listening to the noise of the engine of manual transmission car and know when to change gear.
2. How a heavy vehicle mechanic in a Council depot listens to an engine and is able to determine what may not be working as it should.
3. How a customer service officer in a Council call centre listens for clues in the customer's voice and pace of speech to detect escalating emoting in the interaction.
4. How a development officer can make judgements and provide advice about the compliance of a development application by considering the submitted documentation as well as drawing on knowledge about the local area.

Tacit to tacit knowledge sharing through socialisation occurs when individuals share experiences with each other. In more formal sense such as the 'master-apprentice' model, learning of tacit knowledge occurs through specific instances of observing, imitating and practicing a new skill. In a less formal sense when an existing employee shares knowledge about some aspects of work with other employees through more incidental observations and experiences. For example, when an experienced customer service officer demonstrates to a novice how to detect emotions in callers by letting them listen in on customer calls as they happen. Or, when a junior development officer works alongside a more experienced one and participates in the assessment process. Socialisation may also involve the sharing of feelings and beliefs implicitly in the tacit knowledge being shared. For example, when an experienced development officer may undertake site inspections to test out intuitions regarding the quality and accuracy of documentation submitted as part of an application.

Externalization (tacit to explicit) involves expressing tacit knowledge explicitly in ways others can understand and learn. This could be through the articulation of concepts and models in words or text and what we see in textbooks, procedures and instructions. We make knowledge explicit through various methods including writing and explanation, use of analogies, metaphors and images, through discussion of ideas with others when we ask questions and provide answers and explanations. Externalisation also draws on reflection on what we know and what we might want to know. An example of this may be a mowing maintenance crew writing a procedure for mowing a cricket pitch which differs in some specific ways from mowing a nature strip. The tacit aspects of maintaining a different kind of council assets become explicit and an opportunity for others to come to learn what to do and how to do it differently. Another example in the context of local government is the sharing of practice notes, common in the development and assessment profession (Nonaka, 1991, 2007; Nonaka & Takeuchi, 1995; Nonaka & Von Krogh, 2009; Linderman, 2004).

Combination (explicit to explicit) involves bringing together distinct pieces of knowledge to form new knowledge which may be reformed and recontextualised. This is done through collating and synthesising the various bits of knowledge. For example, when a Council's management accountants bring together various elements of financial information to prepare Council's Financial projections reports; or when strategic town planners put together development control plans by drawing on various existing LIS (land information system) data and relevant State Government policies and then contextualising this information for the local area and audiences. These reports may be considered new knowledge because they provide a new synthesis of already existing organisational bits of knowledge. Though these reports may have the potential to instigate new knowledge creation, this can only happen if they are shared, discussed and used with and by others in the organisation (Nonaka, 1991, 2007; Nonaka & Takeuchi, 1995; Nonaka & Von Krogh, 2009; Linderman, 2004).

Internalisation (explicit to tacit) brings tacit and explicit knowledge together. This happens when individuals internalise explicit knowledge and question and reframe and broaden their own existing tacit knowledge. For example, financial reports generated and shared by Council accountants may trigger new understandings for managers. This can only happen if managers use these bits of knowledge to change their existing understandings of Council finances and their own practice in managing their budgets. As the new knowledge is internalised it becomes normalised and part of accepted understandings and everyday practice of the organisation (Nonaka, 1991, 2007; Nonaka & Takeuchi, 1995; Nonaka & Von Krogh, 2009; Linderman, 2004).

Given the discussion above, it is important to remember that to be effective, engagement in each of the elements of the knowledge-sharing model is necessary. The application of each element needs to be part of everyday work – thus facilitating the movement of knowledge from tacit to explicit – so that each iteration can build on the previous. Through this approach, knowledge of individuals can be shared with others and as part of organisational knowledge sharing practices, which are further taken up, reshaped and enacted as part of organisational practices. 'How we do things around here' therefore becomes 'how we ***now*** do things around here' (Nonaka, 1991, 2007; Nonaka & Takeuchi, 1995; Nonaka & Von Krogh, 2009; Linderman, 2004).

Learning that happens through knowledge-sharing practices therefore has the potential to embed and drive organisational change towards improvements.

Can learning mitigate other barriers to CI?

Given that learning and knowledge sharing play such an important role in CI, can shift the attention towards learning and knowledge sharing in CI practice help organisations to overcome barriers to CI? This is an important question. A useful starting point in answering this question may be to consider barriers to the implementation of CI.

Barriers to the implementation of CI are not unique to local government and have been experienced across various sectors for at least three decades. This suggests that barriers are persistent and difficult to overcome because they challenge the very nature of the ways in which organisation are structured, managed, respond to change and learn. Operating in complex, multi-facetted organisations like local government which are often resource constrained, it is not uncommon for individuals to feel that they simply do not have time or opportunity to engage in knowledge-sharing activities. This may consequently lead to missed opportunities to facilitate learning for others and may impact broader learning driven changes in how something is practiced in the organisation. We have collated and summarised these barriers in Table 3.1. The discussion that follows presents how these barriers may be implicated in limiting knowledge sharing and learning which could potentially emerge from CI.

It is not surprising in contexts where learning is not acknowledged, recognised as a core capability, or valued, that there may be a lack of *commitment* to CI and the associated changes may be feared by managers and employees (Angell & Corbett, 2009; Singh & Singh, 2015; Masters, 1996). This is because CI initiatives inherently require people to be empowered to make changes in existing organisational practices and structures by learning and embedding new bits of knowledge in day-to-day work practices: fundamentals for CI to be realised. CI relies on trust, involvement and engagement of people and openness of existing organisational power structures and practices to bring change. These aspects mirror what is necessary for learning to ensue. Yet this is not always possible because the organisational capacity for enabling learning and change may be inhibited by already existing organisational ways of doing things.

Further, a lack of *commitment*, clarity of *purpose,* a lack of resource investment and short-term financial focus may lead to the use of de-

Table 3.1 A thematic summary of barriers identified in literature reviews spanning 30 years

Barrier	*Singh & Singh (2015)*	*Angell & Corbett (2009)*	*Masters (1996)*
Commitment	Lack of: • Management commitment to CI • Strong motivation • Leadership • Commitment to customer • Management of politics and turf protection	Lack of: • Top management commitment • Vision	Lack of management commitmentLimited commitment to what customers need and expect, resulting in misdirected efforts and investments
People	Lack of: • Real employee empowerment • Employee trust in senior managementResistance of the workforce	Lack of comprehensive staff involvementFear of change	Fear of changeInadequate use of empowerment and teamwork
Purpose	Short-term focus or focus purely on financial resultsView of quality programme as a quick fix	Lack of: • Constancy of purpose/customer • Customer orientation Organizational complacency	Accreditation
Infrastructure	Failure to change organizational philosophy and/or cultureIneffective measurement techniquesUse of an off-the-shelf programmes Lack of: • Formalized strategic plan for change resources and time to	Top-down implementationLack of planning Implementation missteps/mishandlingWork overload/limited resourcesLack of clear measurement system	Inability to change organisational cultureLack of • Open/ non-threatening communication • Clarity in implementation Improper planningIneffective: • Measurement process/ techniques

improvement initiatives or poor/improper planning • Effective measurement of quality improvementPoor communication	• Data management (access/accuracy/reliability) • Use of data/information to support decision makers/drive change in structure/culture/policy

contextualised 'off the shelf' models for CI (Angell & Corbett, 2009; Singh, et al., 2015). In learning terms, this often means that the emphasis is on learning *about* the frameworks (e.g. ABEF, ISO) and the tools within them (i.e. various forms of process mapping, root-cause analysis) at the expense of learning *how* to select and use such tools by drawing on existing organisational bits of knowledge and contextual understandings. This lack of contextualisation can often lead to the underperformance of CI programs, thus positioning CI as a *non-essential organisational activity.* This then may further impact the potential value of CI in facilitating learning and new knowledge creation and the embedding of CI as an organisational core practice.

Ineffectual supporting *infrastructure* to CI including poor measurement and performance management approaches and limited timely and reliable data (Angell & Corbett, 2009) may inhibit learning about how well the organisation is performing. For example, knowledge which may emerge from CI initiatives focused on the understanding customer and stakeholder needs may be difficult to capture and share and therefore may not always utilised to inform strategy development and implementation. This in turn may lead to misdirected efforts and investments that further impact the effectiveness of CI initiatives to create customer value (Masters, 1996). Although seemingly obvious, managers need to learn *how to use* performance feedback (which is a key aspect of learning) to inform priorities regarding which organisational policies, processes and services should be targeted for CI.

How can knowledge sharing support learning in CI practice?

Nonaka (1991) maintains that to better understand knowledge creation in organisations a new focus on knowledge sharing interactions is critical. Such interactions need to become part of the social fibre of the organisation. This at times may appear counter-intuitive. Spending time in interactions with others – taking time out to talk, reflect and challenge current ways of doing things – when experiencing work pressures may seem impossible. However, such actions have the potential to create spaces where tacit and explicit knowledge are brought together to create new value, new understanding and open up the organisation and its people to new possibilities.

When considering tacit to tacit knowledge, sharing day-to-day experiences together with others in the same space physically or virtually (online) is important. Therefore, local government organisations must not only rely on documented job descriptions and procedures for knowing what to do. It must also create opportunities for observation and meaningful discussion about work and work practices as part of day-to-day work. Observations and discussions in the context of tacit knowledge sharing provide insights into work practices which are not possible when relying only on formal documentation. Encouraging the asking of questions about the work practices, its history, rationale and day-to-day impact are critical. This serves to develop understanding as a foundation for further knowledge sharing, knowledge creation and continuous improvement of work practices. These opportunities are not only valuable among employees but also with customers, suppliers, the wider community and other stakeholders. In the context of local government, examples of activities such as job shadowing, community forums and site visits provide opportunities for people to interact and informally listen and see. All of these support tacit knowledge sharing and may lead to improvements in practice. An important element of the tacit to tacit knowledge sharing is the in-situ emergent aspect which needs to be a consideration when using virtual contexts for knowledge sharing.

Making tacit knowledge explicit also requires interactions, but of different kinds. This approach may involve discussions between peers from different departments coming together to solve a problem, work on a project or sharing ideas via virtual means (e.g. discussion boards and messaging apps). This may also involve discussions with customers. For example, duty planners engaging with builders and developers throughout the assessment and approval processes. Such interactions may surface contradictions stemming from different interpretations of the already existing explicit bits of knowledge (e.g. development policies and controls). In surfacing contradictions and moving forward towards an agreement, it is necessary for people to let go of routines that tie them to the already existing practice and to open up to possibilities for new learning in order to create new meanings and understandings.

It is important to recognise that in the context of local government, knowledge sharing and the creation of new meanings often occurs in an 'openly contested environment that needs to take into account power relations and political processes' (Woods, Tan & Ryan, 2015 p.4). These forces may therefore enable or inhibit possibilities for what is shared, what may be discussed, and what new perspectives are possible and acceptable, including changes that may emerge from CI initiatives. Awareness and consideration of how to manage and mitigate the influence of such contestations and political processes are essential for knowledge sharing, creation and learning and facilitate the embedding of CI practice.

Explicit to explicit knowledge sharing (i.e. the combination element of Nonaka's knowledge creation model) is exemplified through organisational documents such as policy and procedures, practice notes, reports and business plans. It can also include associated social processes such as strategic and operational planning, budgeting and community/stakeholder consultations outputs (of which are shared with stakeholders). Sharing these explicit bits of knowledge and embedding stakeholder responses into how the organisation executes such plans provides the opportunity for internalisation and application in practice of the emergent bits of knowledge. The actualisation of business plans into council services and internal operations which are based on these bits of knowledge may add further value to the community and stakeholders. If these processes are predominantly actioned as mandatory requirements of legislation, opportunities for knowledge sharing, creation, learning may be overlooked. This is a pertinent point by Ryan & Hastings (2015) in their work on community involvement in planning and performance measurement development in local government, where opportunities for improvement may be overshadowed by compliance requirements.

It becomes more and more apparent that capacity and opportunities for employees and managers to reflect on existing work practices and consider various forms of knowledge is necessary. However, this may be viewed as a 'nice to have' in the busy lives of local government managers and executives. This may, in some instances, require significant shifts in the cultural value of learning and knowledge sharing and time for reflection. It may mean assisting managers and employees to develop the necessary skills for critical reflection as well as creating the time and space to do so, via mechanisms such as coaching, mentoring, communities of practice or simply incidental connections between peers. This may well be the final aspect not only to consolidate learning and transforming new explicit bits of knowledge into tacit bits of knowledge, as part of the knowledge creation model discussed by Nonaka, but also a key mechanism for embedding CI as a sustainable organisational practice.

Concluding comments

A lack of commitment and a lack of clarity of purpose in the implementation of CI may result in the use of de-contextualised 'off the shelf' models for CI. This risks a shift in emphasis towards learning about frameworks and the tools at the expense of embedding CI as a learning practice in the organisation. When considering the implementation of CI as an organisational program, it is important for local government organisations to revisit well-established quality and continuous improvement philosophies such as Kaizan which consider the facilitation of learning and knowledge sharing as both a driver and outcome of CI.

We propose that the Organisational Knowledge Creation Theory (OKCT) and knowledge sharing framework (Nonaka, 1991; Nonaka and Toyama, 2015) discussed in this chapter. It provides an accessible research-informed framework that can be used by practitioners to ensure 'workers' experiences, learnings, and acquired knowledge are inherited accumulatively and shared' (Nakamori, 2019 p. 273) with others as part of a collective approach to learning and working. This in turn can inform organisational structures, systems and ways of working. It is clear that knowledge creation occurs through situated actions and reflection with others. An organisational context that values internal and external engagement and interactions, and relationship building amongst its people and stakeholders are critical for establishing a conducive environment for learning and embedding CI.

Notes

1 ABEF/ISO were integrated when ISO purchased the ABEF IP.
2 Refer to the Appendix for a summary of definitions from Sanchez & Blanco (2014).

References

Angell, L.C. and Corbett, L.M. 2009. The quest for business excellence: Evidence from New Zealand's award winners. *International Journal of Operations & Production Management*, *29*(2), pp. 170–199. https://doi.org/10.1108/01443570910932048

Bhuiyan, N. and Baghel, A. 2005. An overview of continuous improvement: From the past to the present. *Management Decision*, *43*(5), pp. 761–771. https://doi.org/10.1108/00251740510597761

Carnerud, D., Jaca, C. and Bäckström, I. 2018. Kaizen and continuous improvement–trends and patterns over 30 years. *The TQM Journal*, *30*(4), pp.371–390. https://doi.org/10.1108/TQM-03-2018-0037

Fryer, K.J., Antony, J. and Douglas, A. 2007. Critical success factors of continuous improvement in the public sector. *The TQM Magazine*, *19*(5), pp. 497–517. https://doi.org/10.1108/09544780710817900

Imai, M. 1986. *Kaizen: The key to Japan's competitive success*. McGraw-Hill Education, New York.

Jurburg, D., Viles, E., Tanco, M. and Mateo, R. 2017. What motivates employees to participate in continuous improvement activities?. *Total Quality Management & Business Excellence*, *28*(13-14), pp. 1469–1488. https://doi.org/10.1080/14783363.2016.1150170

Kovach, J.V. and Fredendall, L.D. 2013. The influence of continuous improvement practices on learning: An empirical study. *Quality Management Journal*, *20*(4), pp. 6–20. https://doi.org/10.1080/10686967.2013.11918361

Kovach, J.V. and Fredendall, L.D. 2014. Managerial impacts of learning and continuous improvement practices. *The Journal for Quality and Participation*, *37*(2), p. 25.

Kovach, J.V. and Fredendall, L.D. 2015. Learning during design for six sigma projects—A preliminary investigation in behavioral healthcare. *Engineering Management Journal*, *27*(3), pp. 109–123. https://doi.org/10.1080/10429247.2015.1047478

Letmathe, P., Schweitzer, M. and Zielinski, M. 2012. How to learn new tasks: Shop floor performance effects of knowledge transfer and performance feedback. *Journal of Operations Management*, *30*(3), pp. 221–236. https://doi.org/10.1016/j.jom.2011.11.001

Linderman, K., Schroeder, R.G., Zaheer, S., Liedtke, C. and Choo, A.S. 2004. Integrating quality management practices with knowledge creation processes. *Journal of Operations Management*, *22*(6), pp. 589–607. https://doi.org/10.1016/j.jom.2004.07.001

Masters, R.J. 1996. Overcoming the barriers to TQM's success. *Quality Progress*, *29*(5), p. 53.

Nakamori, T., Takahashi, K., Han, B.T. and McIver, D. 2019. Understanding KAIZEN practice in Japanese overseas manufacturing: A framework. *International Journal of Knowledge Management Studies*, *10*(3), pp. 271–298. https://doi.org/10.1504/IJKMS.2019.101481

Nonaka, I. 1991. The knowledge-creating company. *Harvard Business Review*, *69*(6), pp. 96–104.

Nonaka, I. and Takeuchi, H. 2007. The knowledge-creating company. *Harvard Business Review*, *85*(7/8), pp. 162–171.

Nonaka, I. and Takeuchi, H. 1995. *The knowledge-creating company: How Japanese companies create the dynamics of innovation*. Oxford University Press, Oxford/New York

Nonaka, I. and Toyama, R. 2015. The Knowledge-creating Theory Revisited: Knowledge Creation as a Synthesizing Process. In: Edwards, J.S. (ed.), *The Essentials of Knowledge Management*. OR Essentials Series. Palgrave Macmillan, London. https://doi.org/10.1057/9781137552105_4

Nonaka, I. and Von Krogh, G. 2009. Perspective—Tacit knowledge and knowledge conversion: Controversy and advancement in organizational knowledge creation theory. *Organization Science*, *20*(3), pp. 635–652. https://doi.org/10.1287/orsc.1080.0412

Ramírez, K.A. and Álvaro, V.P. 2017. Continuous improvement practices with Kaizen approach in companies of the metropolitan district of Quito: An exploratory study. *Intangible Capital*, *13*(2), pp. 479–497. https://doi.org/10.3926/ic.901

Ryan, R. and Hastings, C. 2015. Missed opportunities for democratic engagement: The adoption of community indicators in local government. *Asia Pacific Journal of Public Administration*, *37*(1), pp. 33–43. https://doi.org/10.1080/23276665.2015.1018376

Sanchez, L. and Blanco, B. 2014. Three decades of continuous improvement. *Total Quality Management & Business Excellence*, *25*(9–10), pp. 986–1001. https://doi.org/10.1080/14783363.2013.856547

Singh, J. and Singh, H. 2015. Continuous improvement philosophy–literature review and directions. *Benchmarking: An International Journal*, *22*(1), pp. 75–119. https://doi.org/10.1108/BIJ-06-2012-0038

Suárez-Barraza, M.F., Ramis-Pujol, J. and Kerbache, L. 2011. Thoughts on kaizen and its evolution: Three different perspectives and guiding principles. *International Journal of Lean Six Sigma*, *2*(4), pp. 288–308. https://doi.org/10.1108/20401461111189407.

Woods, R., Tan, S. and Ryan, R. 2015. Councils learning from each other: An Australian case study, Australian Centre of Excellence for Local Government, University of Technology Sydney, Australia.

4 Case study #1 Stakeholder analysis for continuous improvement — A New Zealand perspective

Understanding stakeholders and stakeholder analysis in local government

'Stakeholder' is a common term in everyday business dialogue as well as a commonly used term in the everyday professional conversations of local government organisations. However, while there is a tendency to use this term as part of day-to-day conversations, the term stakeholder has a specific and theorised meaning associated with it. For example, according to the classic definition of Freeman (2010), stakeholders are '*any group or individual who can affect or is affected by the achievement of the organisation's objectives*' (p. 46). Stakeholder management is vital for the successful planning and implementation of continuous improvement initiatives in local government organisations.

A local government organisation can affect or is affected by a variety of stakeholder groups in their continuous improvement initiatives. Typical examples of such stakeholders include community, councillors, employees, suppliers, media and other local councils. Within these broad stakeholder groups, there can be subgroups as well as individual stakeholders. Some studies have found that since the continuous improvement projects of local councils exist in the public domain, the stakeholders of the projects may feel that they have a right to be involved in the decision-making process because they will be affected by the ultimate policy choice (Elias & Zwikael, 2007).

In this context, managing the stakeholders of a local government organisation is no easy task. First, there are many groups or individuals who can be regarded as stakeholders of a continuous improvement project initiated by a local council. In addition to the sheer number of stakeholders, many of them can have conflicting stakes. That is, while one stakeholder has one interest or stake, another stakeholder can have an exactly opposite interest or stake. For example, a

DOI: 10.4324/9781003011675-4

supplier of a local council may be interested in charging more as per the market rate for its services while many members of the community may oppose any extra spending by the Council. Therefore, there is an inherent complexity in managing multiple stakeholders with conflicting stakes.

Another aspect that makes stakeholder management more difficult is the changing positions and interests of stakeholders over time. For example, a particular stakeholder may have supported a continuous improvement project involving the construction of an infrastructure asset prior to Covid-19. However, the same stakeholder may be less supportive or opposite the expenditure when revised financial information is assessed due to the situation being faced by a region as a result of the impact of the pandemic. This means that stakeholder management in a local council is not just complex, it can also be dynamic (Mitchell, et al., 1997). This example illustrates the importance for the managers of continuous improvement projects in local councils to identify and analyse the stakeholders of the project so as to manage them effectively.

In the section that follows, a stakeholder analysis framework is introduced. The framework may be used in various organisational situations and programs including continuous improvement projects in local councils.

Overview of stakeholder theory

The stakeholder concept first appeared in the management literature in 1963, when the word was used in an international memorandum at the Stanford Research Institute (Freeman, 2010). Stakeholders were then defined *'as those groups without whose support the organisation would cease to exist'*. Several other definitions have appeared in the management literature since 1963, but definitions provided by Freeman (2010) and Clarkson (1995) are still used by many experts in their work. Freeman's definition, that was presented in the previous section, is considered as a broad definition of stakeholders while Clarkson's definition is seen as providing a narrower perspective focusing predominantly on risk, identifying stakeholders as voluntary or involuntary risk-bearers. Voluntary stakeholders bear some form of risk as a result of having invested some form of capital, human or financial, something of value, in an organisation. Involuntary stakeholders are placed at risk as a result of an organisation's activities. According to Clarkson (1995), without the element of risk, there is no stake.

The evolution of stakeholder theory was captured by some researchers in the field (e.g. Elias, 2019): after its origin in 1963, the stakeholder concept diversified into four different fields, namely: corporate planning, systems theory, corporate social responsibility and organisation theory. The next landmark in the development of stakeholder theory is the classic book by Freeman (2010), *Strategic Management: A Stakeholder Approach* that was first published in 1984. After this book, the stakeholder literature developed around three different aspects, namely: descriptive aspect, instrumental aspect and normative aspect. Donaldson & Preston (1995) brought these three aspects together in their stakeholder theory of corporation. Later, the stakeholder literature started spreading its wings to interesting areas like dynamics of stakeholders (Mitchell, et al., 1997) and stakeholder networking (Rowley, 1997). Several theoretical approaches (e.g. Friedman & Miles, 2002) and empirical studies (Elias, 2017) also followed. Today, the stakeholder literature is still evolving with theoretical developments and empirical studies.

The book by Freeman which he first published in 1984 and then in 2010 is worth mentioning at this point. The main contribution of the book is in providing a framework for analysing stakeholders of an organisation. This framework consists of three levels of analysis – rational, process and transactional. The rational level analysis includes the identification of stakeholders and their stakes while in the process level the processes used by the organisation to deal with the stakeholders are analysed. The transactional level analysis addresses the effectiveness of transactions between the firm and the stakeholders. Based on the rational, process and transactional level analysis the *Stakeholder Management Capability* of a firm can also be determined.

In addition to Freeman's framework, several other models and frameworks appear in the stakeholder literature that can aid the analysis of stakeholders in a continuous improvement project. One such example is a stakeholder typology model developed by Mitchell et al. (1997). This model is based on the three attributes: power, legitimacy and urgency. According to their typology (Table 4.1), if a stakeholder possesses only one of the three attributes, they are termed latent stakeholders and have low stakeholder salience. If the only attribute present is power, such stakeholders are called dormant stakeholders; if it is only legitimacy, they are called discretionary stakeholders and if only urgency, they are called demanding stakeholders. Stakeholder salience will be moderate, if two attributes are present and such stakeholders are called expectant stakeholders. Among the expectant stakeholders, those having power and legitimacy only are called dominant stakeholders; those having

Table 4.1 Stakeholder typology model

Attributes	*Stakeholder type*	*Stakeholder name*
Power only	Latent	Dormant stakeholder
Legitimacy only	Latent	Discretionary stakeholder
Urgency only	Latent	Demanding stakeholder
Power and legitimacy only	Expectant	Dominant stakeholder
Legitimacy and urgency only	Expectant	Dependent stakeholder
Power and urgency only	Expectant	Dangerous stakeholder
Power legitimacy and urgency	Definitive	Definitive stakeholder

legitimacy and urgency only are called dependent stakeholders and those having power and urgency only are called dangerous stakeholders. Stakeholder salience will be high where all three attributes are perceived by managers to be present in a stakeholder. In such a case they are called definitive stakeholders. Furthermore, this model also shows the dynamic qualities of stakeholders. This is because stakeholders can be recategorized from one class to another, when the salience of stakeholders increase/decrease by attaining/losing one or more of the attributes.

This chapter will propose and illustrate a stakeholder analysis framework combining the works of Freeman (2010) and Mitchell et al. (1997).

A New Zealand case

Katy (name disguised) is an MBA graduate of Victoria University of Wellington. Prior to joining the MBA, she gained almost six years of professional experience in central government, working for a ministry in Wellington and climbing the ladder to become a lead advisor there. During the final stages of her MBA, Katy had her first child, while securing a role with the local council in the greater Wellington area. She started as a team lead and in three years became an acting director. During this time, Katy and her husband welcomed their second child and wanting to continue to work as close to home as possible while her children were young, she joined another nearby local council as a Business Improvement Manager. This council, based in the centre of a small town in the North Island of New Zealand, consists of an elected Mayor, 10 councillors and is run by the support of a 7-member Strategic Leadership Team (SLT) led by the Chief Executive of the Council.

During the first five weeks of her work at the Council, Katy engaged with stakeholders conducting over 40 interviews with staff in the Council. This included all staff in tier two positions and their direct reports. The objective was to identify opportunities to improve processes and systems. Based on these conversations, she identified three common themes for continuous improvement and reported them to the SLT. They included (i) Information management – refining information management processes, including automating some manual processes. (ii) Leadership – Standardising approaches to coaching and performance management, meeting format and frequency, communication and dissemination of information; Encouraging SLT members to delegate more and empower direct reports; Refining SLT governance practices will enable better co-ordination of organisational work planning, and mitigate reactive, unplanned work. (iii) Organisation – reviewing resource allocation to ensure that departments are resourced sufficiently and appropriately; revising job descriptions to ensure they are comprehensive and up to date; ensuring clarity and specificity in relation to job titles and areas of responsibility; and enhancing customer centricity in departments not traditionally thought of as customer service oriented, including the development of internal and external service level agreements, with clearly articulated expectations and performance indicators, to monitor and support this.

In addition to these three broad themes, Katy also integrated a list of business improvement initiatives provided by the SLT into her continuous improvement programme. At this point, she realised that there was tension between quick wins, addressing short-term problems, and investing in sustainable solutions to strategic problems. She decided to meet with the SLT and operational staff to regularly review and revalidate her continuous improvement priorities.

Katy developed a business improvement work programme that scheduled dedicated time to review processes that existed within each corporate group at the Council. The first team to benefit from this review was the Building team. Katy sat with the Building team for four weeks, and even purchased a pair of steel-capped boots so that she could shadow the building inspectors and go out with them on site visits. She interviewed each team member and collated feedback about processes and systems that were working well, and those that needed to be reviewed. Once she had developed a list of improvement opportunities, she facilitated a workshop with key members of the team to develop an action plan. Team members were tasked with the actions and the action plan was passed to the incoming Team Leader for ongoing management.

Another key priority Katy had to take care of was the Local Government New Zealand's CouncilMARK™ programme on behalf of the Council. The CouncilMARK™ programme is designed to improve the public's knowledge of the work councils are doing in their communities and to support individual councils to further improve the service and value they provide. The programme incorporates an independent assessment system that assesses how councils are performing and the work they're undertaking to grow the value they deliver. Councils receive an overall performance rating from an Independent Assessment Board and commentary on their performance.

The four priorities areas for CouncilMARK™ are: (i) excellence in governance, leadership and strategy; (ii) excellence and transparency in financial decision-making; (iii) excellence in service delivery and asset management; and (iv) strong engagement with the public and businesses. Co-ordinating the assessment, including completing a comprehensive self-assessment, takes considerable time and resource. Katy was tasked with co-ordinating the Council's second assessment (due March 2020) on behalf of the SLT. This included capturing changes and improvements made to date in relation to recommendations from the initial assessment. This update was also to be made available to the Audit and Risk Committee of the Council.

At this juncture, Katy realised that there are several stakeholders who could affect the success of the Councils' continuous improvement journey. She also had some important questions in her mind:

- Who are the main stakeholders of the Council's continuous improvement programme? How can I know them better before I proceed with any continuous improvement initiatives?
- What are the processes that the council use to consult, communicate or deal with these stakeholders? How efficient are these processes?
- How effective are the negotiations and transactions between the Council and these stakeholders?
- Who are the stakeholders who support or oppose a (particular) continuous improvement project? How can I better understand their positions?
- Have the stakeholders changed their positions over time? How can I understand such changes?

The following sections aim at addressing Katy's questions by presenting a stakeholder analysis framework and applying it to some of her continuous improvement initiatives.

Stakeholder analysis framework

The stakeholder analysis framework discussed is based on the existing literature discussed in section 2. Specifically, it is based on the works of Freeman (2010), Mitchell et al. (1997), Elias (2016) and Elias (2017). The stakeholder analysis framework consists of six phases as shown in Figure 4.1.

The *rational level phase* involves the identification of the stakeholders of the CI project and their perceived stakes. *The process level phase* is about understanding how the CI project management implicitly or explicitly manages its relationships with its stakeholders. The transactional level aims at understanding the set of transactions or bargains between the project management and its stakeholders and deduce whether these negotiations fit with the stakeholder map and the organisational processes for stakeholders. The management capability phase is about the determination of stakeholder management capability of the CI project, based on the rational, process and

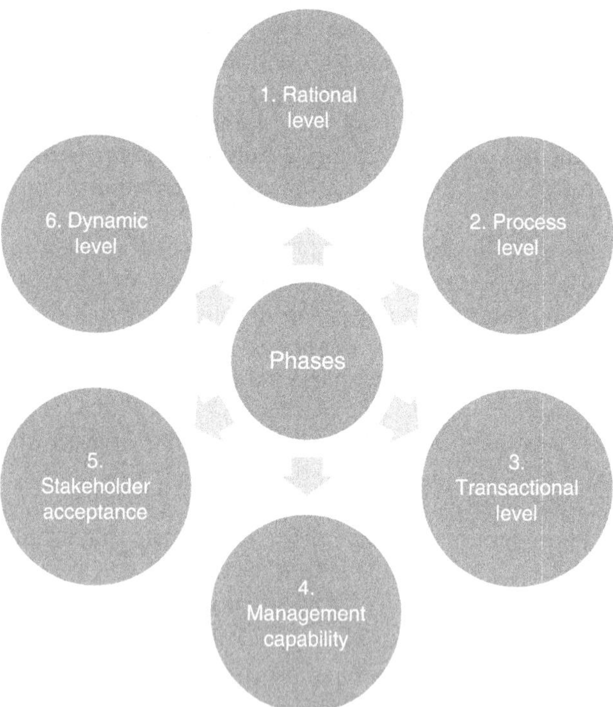

Figure 4.1 Stakeholder analysis framework.

Table 4.2 Stakeholder analysis framework

Phases	*Steps*
1 Rational level	1 Develop a stakeholder map for the CI project 2 Prepare a chart of specific stakeholders for the CI project 3 Identify the stakes of stakeholders of the CI project 4 Prepare a power versus stake grid for the CI project
2 Process level	6 Conduct a process level stakeholder analysis for the CI project
3 Transactional level	7 Conduct a transactional level stakeholder analysis for the CI project
4 Management capability	8 Determine the stakeholder management capability for the CI project
5 Stakeholder acceptance	9 Analyse the acceptance of stakeholders to the CI project
6 Dynamic level	10 Analyse the salience of stakeholders of the CI project

transactional levels of stakeholder analysis. The next phase of stakeholder acceptance involves the analysis of acceptance by the different stakeholders affected by the CI project. The final phase dynamic level consists of analysing the dynamics of stakeholders using the model developed by Mitchell et al. (1997).

Table 4.2 shows each phase and lists the steps in each phase. The next section illustrates this framework by applying it to the case presented in section 3.

Illustration of stakeholder analysis to the case

As shown in Table 4.2, the first phase of rational level stakeholder analysis consists of four steps.

1 Develop a stakeholder map for the CI project

The first step is to develop a stakeholder map that includes stakeholder groups who can or are affected by the CI project. A stakeholder map for the project is shown in Figure 4.2.

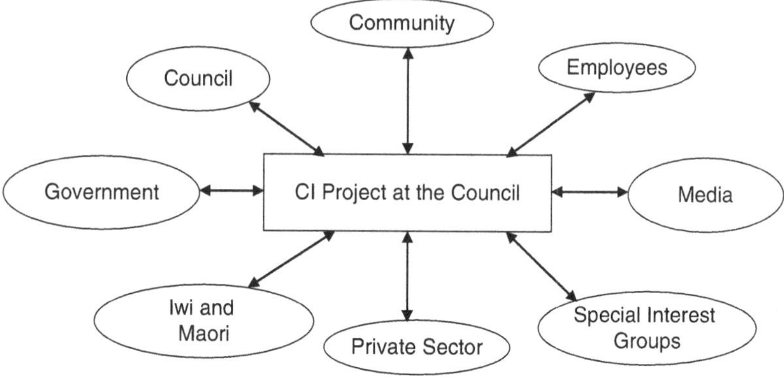

Figure 4.2 Stakeholder map.

2 Prepare a chart of specific stakeholders for the CI project

The second step in the rational level analysis is to prepare a chart of specific stakeholders. This chart identifies the specific stakeholders by expanding the stakeholder groups identified in the stakeholder map. For the CI Project, the specific stakeholder is shown in Table 4.3.

3 Identify the stakes of stakeholders of the CI project

As the third step in the rational level stakeholder analysis, the stakes of the specific stakeholder groups of the CI project are identified and analysed. Table 4.4 shows the stakes of some selected stakeholders of the CI Project at the Council

4 Identify the stakes of stakeholders of the CI project

In the fourth step of the rational level analysis, a two-dimensional grid is prepared. The first dimension categorises the stakeholders by stake while the second dimension by power. Freeman (2010) categorises stakes as equity stake, economic stake and influencer stake; and power into formal or voting power, economic power and political power. For the CI project at the Council, this power versus stake grid for some selected stakeholders is presented in Table 4.5. For example, the Chief Executive was evaluated to have equity stake and formal power.

Table 4.3 Specific stakeholders

Council	*Community*
Mayor Councillors Iwi representatives	Urban rate paying community Rural rate paying community Costal rate paying community
Employees	*Media*
Chief Executive Senior leadership team (SLT) Managers Other staff Public Service Association (PSA)	Wairarapa Times Age Wairarapa's MORE FM 89.5 Stuff.co.nz TVNZ TV 3 Social media
Special Interest Groups	*Private Sector*
Researchers & Academics in Universities Consulting firms Community Groups Service Providers Contractors Society of Local Government Managers (SOLGM)	Viticulture/ Horticulture Agriculture/primary food production Dairy Value Added Food and Beverage Forestry
Iwi and Maori	*Government*
Rangitāne o Wairarapa Kahungunu ki Wairarapa Ngāti Kahungunu ki Wairarapa Tamaki Nui a Rua Treaty Settlement Trust Rangitāne Tū Mai Rā	NZ Parliament Department of Internal Affairs Local Government Commission Local Government New Zealand (LGNZ) Greater Wellington Regional Council Other City Councils

5 *Conduct a process level stakeholder analysis for the CI project*

In the fifth step, an analysis of the processes used by the Council to consult, communicate, or deal with the stakeholders of the CI project was conducted (Zwikael, et al., 2012). This analysis found that as a public sector entity, the Council mainly used formal communications mechanisms for public consultations. There is a dedicated Marketing and Communications team and media releases, website, email, Facebook, other social media were all used to communicate with the stakeholders.

Table 4.4 Stakes of selected stakeholders

Chief Executive of the Council	*Urban Ratepaying Community*
Advise the Council on policy, manage the Council's total operations and be the link between the elected members and the staff	Expectation that adequate resources are spent in the community that will benefit the whole community. The majority of ratepayers do not agree with continued and seemingly high rate rises year on year.
Councillors	*Researchers in Universities*
Represent constituents and community	Research and teaching of CI topics
Local Government New Zealand	*The Wairarapa Times Age*
Represent the national interests of councils in New Zealand and lead best practice in the local government sector.	Maintain/increase readership Generate interest through news stories focussed on Council and its activities. Communicate success stories and criticise failures.

Table 4.5 Power versus stake grid

Power Stake	*Formal or Voting*	*Economic*	*Political*
Equity	Chief Executive		
Economic		Urban Ratepaying Community	
Influencers	NZ Parliament		Wairarapa Times Age

However, it was found that many of the teams worked in silos and therefore internal communication was inefficient and became an impediment for managing the CI programmes at the Council. Additionally, while the Council had communication mechanisms with some of its powerful stakeholders, planned consultation mechanisms were weak or non-existent for some other stakeholders listed in the stakeholder map.

6 Conduct a transactional level stakeholder analysis for the CI project

As the sixth step, an analysis of the effectiveness of transactions and negotiations between the Council and the stakeholders of the CI project was conducted. Successful transactions with stakeholders are built on understanding the legitimacy of the stakeholder and having processes to routinely surface their concerns.

In the Council, implementing the recommendations of the CI project was not an easy task. For example, towards the end of a CI project restructuring of one position was recommended as an action point. This resulted in strong backlash from a group of employees. After some negotiations with the employees, it was decided to withdraw this recommendation. Lack of efficient consultation mechanisms at the process level and some sections in the council working as silos also contribute to such ineffective transactions.

7 Determine the stakeholder management capability for the CI project

The eighth step is to determine the stakeholder management capability of the CI project, based on the rational, process and transactional level analysis of the project. Stakeholder management capability can be defined as its understanding or conceptual map of its stakeholders, the processes for dealing with these stakeholders and the transactions which it uses to carry out the achievement of project purpose with its stakeholders (Freeman, 2010). To determine the stakeholder management capability, first, a judgement on whether the project management understands its stakeholder map or not has to be made. This is followed by a rating of the CI project for the efficiency of its organisational process and the effectiveness of its transactions for dealing with its stakeholders.

According to this analysis of the CI programme at the Council, the programme has a good understanding of their stakeholder map. They can identify the different stakeholders who can or are affected by the programme. For some of the stakeholders in their stakeholder map, they have efficient consultation processes while for some others, especially those who do not hold much power, processes were missing or weak. The effectiveness of transactions was also found in need of improvement since the programme struggled to negotiate conflicting stakes of its stakeholders. Based on this analysis, the stakeholder management capability of this CI project is in Figure 4.3.

8 Analyse the acceptance of stakeholders to the CI project

The ninth step in this stakeholder analysis framework involves the analysis of acceptance by the different stakeholders affected by the CI project. One way of analysing stakeholder acceptance is by developing an acceptance

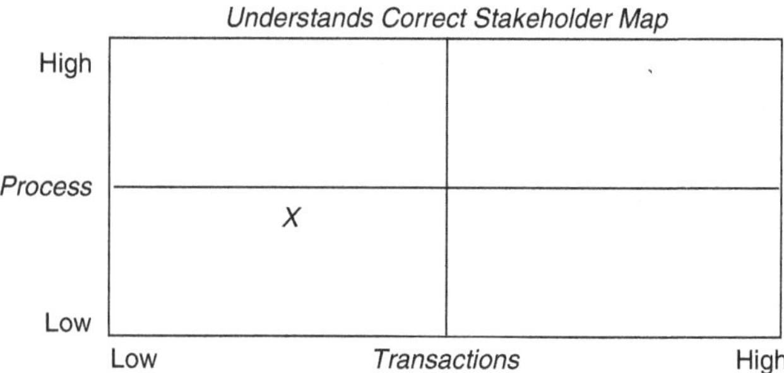

Figure 4.3 Stakeholder management capability index.

Table 4.6 Stakeholder acceptance table

Stakeholders	*Supportive*	*Neutral*	*Opposed*
Chief Executive of the Council	+ +		
SLT of the Council	++		
Mayor of the Council	+		
External Developers	+		
Researchers in Universities		0	
Consulting firms		0	
Public Service Association			-
Some employees of Planning and Building team			-
Employee whose job is restructured			--

table for stakeholder acceptability of individual stakeholders towards the CI project. Such an acceptance table can be developed by listing the key stakeholders in the first column and by assessing whether they are supportive, neutral or opposed. A stakeholder acceptance table for the CI project related to the Building team at the Council is shown in Table 4.6.

9 Analyse the salience of stakeholders of the CI project

The salience of stakeholders in a CI project can change with respect to time. The last phase in this stakeholder analysis framework involves an analysis of this stakeholder dynamics. The stakeholder typology model developed by Mitchell et al. (1997) was used for this purpose. According to this model, the salience of stakeholders can change when their power, legitimacy and urgency changes. It is recommended that CI project

Table 4.7 Stakeholder salience

Dormant (Power only)	*Discretionary (Legitimacy only)*	*Demanding (Urgency only)*	*Dominant (Power & Legitimacy)*
	Researchers & Academics in Universities Consulting firms		NZ Parliament
Dangerous (Power & Urgency)	*Dependent (Legitimacy & Urgency)*	*Definitive (Power, Legitimacy & Urgency)*	*Non-stakeholder (No Power, Legitimacy or Urgency)*
	Rangitāne o Wairarapa Kahungunu ki Wairarapa Wairarapa Times Age Wairarapa's MORE FM 89.5	Chief Executive Senior Leadership Team	

managers continuously update this typology model to capture this dynamic of stakeholders. Table 4.7 presents the salience of some of the stakeholders of the CI project at the Council as an example.

Concluding comments

Stakeholders play a crucial part in the success of a CI project in any local council. Therefore, it is important to identify the stakeholder and their stakes, analyse the processes and transactions used to manage them, and to understand their changing positions and interests towards a CI project. This chapter introduced a stakeholder analysis framework consisting of 10 steps and illustrated it by applying it to a CI project in a local council in New Zealand.

Business improvement managers like Katy may find this tool useful. To use some of her own words 'I learnt that managing a CI project without conducting an in-depth stakeholder analysis can be risky. We may spend a lot of time, effort and money to improve an inefficient process in a council using a CI project, but if the recommendations generate unexpected negative side effects and opposition from the stakeholders, the whole exercise can become ineffective and counter-productive. We may take two steps forward and three steps backward.' Knowing your stakeholders and being prepared to manage them can go a long way in the success of a CI project.

Local council professionals who may use the stakeholder analysis framework presented in the chapter are reminded that it is only a management tool. Its application must be context specific and should be adapted to the CI improvement project that you are managing. In addition, every management tool has strengths as well as weaknesses. For example, while this stakeholder analysis provides a systematic, step-by-step approach it is no way a complete tool for stakeholder analysis. In many situations, this tool may have to be combined with other management tools.

References

Clarkson, M.E. 1995. A stakeholder framework for analyzing and evaluating corporate social performance. *Academy of Management Review*, *20*(1), pp. 92–117. https://doi.org/10.2307/258888

Donaldson, T. and Preston, L.E. 1995. The stakeholder theory of the corporation: Concepts, evidence, and implications. *Academy of Management Review*, *20*(1), pp. 65–91. https://doi.org/10.5465/amr.1995.9503271992

Elias, A.A. and Zwikael, O. 2007. Stakeholder participation in project management: A New Zealand study. Proceedings of the 5th Annual Australian and New Zealand Academy of Management Operations Management Symposium, Melbourne, Australia.

Elias, A.A. 2016. Stakeholder analysis for lean six sigma project management. *International Journal of Lean Six Sigma*, *7*(4), pp. 394–405. https://doi.org/10.1108/IJLSS-11-2015-0046

Elias, A.A. 2017. Systems thinking and modelling for stakeholder management. *IIM Kozhikode Society & Management Review*, *6*(2), pp. 123–131. https://doi.org/10.1177%2F2277975216681105

Elias, A.A. 2019. Strategy development through stakeholder involvement: A New Zealand study. *Global Journal of Flexible Systems Management*, *20*(4), pp. 313–322. https://doi.org/10.1007/s40171-019-00217-6

Freeman, R.E. 2010. *Strategic management: A stakeholder approach*. Cambridge University Press, New York.

Friedman, A.L. and Miles, S. 2002. Developing stakeholder theory. *Journal of Management Studies*, *39*(1), pp. 1–21. https://doi.org/10.1111/1467-6486.00280

Mitchell, R.K., Agle, B.R. and Wood, D.J. 1997. Toward a theory of stakeholder identification and salience: Defining the principle of who and what really counts. *Academy of Management Review*, *22*(4), pp. 853–886. https://doi.org/10.5465/amr.1997.9711022105

Rowley, Timothy J. 1997. Moving beyond dyadic ties: A network theory of stakeholder influences. *Academy of Management Review*, *22*, pp. 887–910.

Zwikael, O., Elias, A.A. and Ahn, M. 2012. Stakeholder collaboration and engagement in virtual projects. *International Journal of Networking and Virtual Organisations*, *10*(2), pp. 117–136. https://doi.org/10.1504/IJNVO.2012.045730

5 Case study #2 in the Australian context – Developing a performance measurement framework in a council undergoing growth

Case study overview and project drivers

The case study describes a project undertaken as part of an industry engagement partnership between the authors and a local government organisation. The local government partner (hereon referred to as '*Municipal*') is a peri-urban council in the outer rim of the Sydney metropolitan area. The local area encompasses rural and agricultural landscape as well as towns and villages, large areas of natural bushland and large-scale infrastructure. This local government area, alongside neighbouring Councils has been recognised as part of the greater Sydney growth corridor.

There were three key contextual drivers for the organisation to prioritise this project. The first contextual driver stemmed from the New South Wales government's *A Metropolis of Three Cities – The Greater Sydney Region Plan* (The Greater Western Sydney Commission Plan, 2018). NSW local governments – like interstate counterparts, operate in contexts where the State and Territorial governments, through various policy instruments, seek to influence 'composition, quality and quantity of services provided' (Dollery, Grant & Kortt, 2013 p. 216) at the local level.

The organisation recognised that to respond to the imperatives of the Greater Sydney Region plan, it had to build organisational capacity in strategic and operational management. Strategic and operational management, through the development of robust performance management and measurement (PMM), is recognised by various authors as critical in achieving effectiveness in service delivery and sustainability (Andrews & Van de Walle, 2013; Baird, Schoch & Chen, 2012; Johnsson, Pepper, Price & Richardson, 2021).

The second driver resulted from the organisation's continuous improvement program, which recognised that to advance the achievement of strategic outcomes, greater alignment was needed between the

DOI: 10.4324/9781003011675-5

integrated planning process and the day-to-day operations. The development of a PMM framework was identified as a key mechanism to drive alignment between strategic and operational outcomes (Nath & Sudharshan, 1994; Boston & Pallot, 1997; Joshi, Kathuria & Porth, 2003; Poister, 2010).

Finally, the executive team in partnership with the elected Council sought to improve the mechanism for reporting progress against the community strategic plan imperatives. Engaging all levels of the organisation's management (including the elected Council) in setting expectations for the PMM framework was a key step in its design. Existing literature recognises that developing a PMM is challenging due to different stakeholders' needs, understandings and application of performance information in their decision making (Pollitt, 2018). This was an important aspect of *Municipal's* approach as they recognised different emerging needs and expectations at the inception of the process.

At the time of the project *Municipal* had a solid footing in the planning aspects of the NSW Integrated Planning and Reporting Framework (NSW Office of Local Government, 2020). The further refinement between planning, measurement and reporting was needed to achieve stronger alignment and prioritisation that reflected the resource investment and work done for the community. This particular project is situated in a larger body of work undertaken by *Municipal* aiming to build capacity and respond sustainably during a period of growth context.

Given this background, the overarching aim of the project was to develop a contextualised performance management framework and associated measures to inform operational and strategic planning. In addition, building of performance measurement and management capability in the organisation was also recognised as an aim of this project. Specifically, the objectives of the project were:

- Evaluate existing organisational approaches to performance measurement and reporting to identify gaps;
- work with the operational management team to develop and embed the performance measurement competencies;
- identifying performance measures to reflect the work of operational units delivering service to the community;
- linking performance measures to the existing planning framework.

The project began with a broad engagement strategy aiming to build understanding about organisational expectations and capabilities. This was achieved through a series of workshops and interviews with councillors, executives, managers, and business unit team leaders. This initial step was important because it facilitated the capture of stakeholder's expectations and understandings about the project and provided insights into the detailed project design and planning. Detailed project planning took place in partnership with the organisation's executive, project sponsor and project officer as a precursor to the initial framework design.

Conceptualising the performance measurement and management (PMM) framework

The development of a PMM framework may be considered an iterative and cyclical process, encompassing three core elements: *Strategic prioritisation*, *articulation of outcome indicator*s and *definition of operational activities* and *performance measures*. Strategic prioritisation focuses on identifying and describing the core outcomes (what) and strategies (how) that are the focus for the planning period. The articulation of outcome indicators relates to the development of key performance indicators for the core outcomes. The definition of operational activities and performance measures element focuses on capturing, defining and identifying the operational activities and associated measures. It is critical the relationships between operational activities and strategic outcomes and performance measures and KPIs, are clearly articulated (Melnyk, et al., 2005). Working through each of these elements is dynamic and ongoing as the organisation responds to external contextual changes and internal improvements.

Due to the cyclical nature of the framework, any one of the core elements may be used as a starting point for the development of the organisation's tailored performance measurement and management framework. The initial application of the framework provides a means of orientation to the level of an organisation's maturity in each core element. The assessment which emerges from the initial application and the organisation's recognised pressure points are used to inform decision making regarding which of the core elements is the most appropriate starting point.

The foundations for developing a PMM Framework are depicted in Figure 5.1.

Another way to depict the framework is by considering the relationship between key performance indicators, lag and lead measure that are associated with the achievement of strategic outcomes, key process outcomes and core activities. This is shown in Figure 5.2.

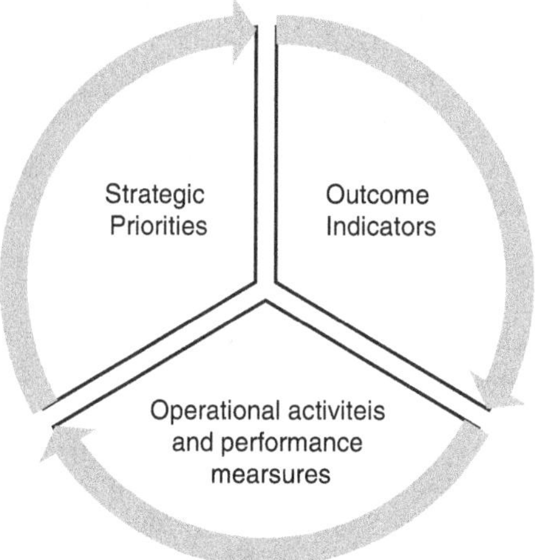

Figure 5.1 Foundations for a performance measurement and management framework adapted from Melnyk et al. (2005 p. 175).

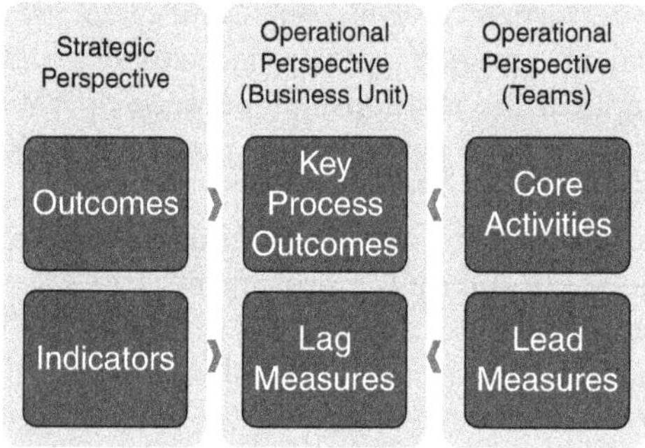

Figure 5.2 Conceptual structure of PMM.

Putting the conceptual PMM framework into practice

Initial engagement and organisational analysis

At *Municipal* the initial assessment commenced with discussions with internal stakeholders to identify the organisation's expectations, understandings and self-assed pressure points and expectations. The next stage analysed existing strategic and operational plans and any associated KPIs and measures. Other documents were analysed including existing performance reports (both external and internal) and business unit operational frameworks and activities. This initial analysis focused on understanding the strategic planning process and its relationship to performance measurement and management. This facilitated our orientation to the organisation and its priorities and the organisational planning and measurement practices.

Outcomes from initial organisational and document analysis

In considering the strategic outcome indicators and measures presented in the short and medium-term plans and performance reports we found that these showed limited articulation of cross-functional work and complexity of achieving expected outcomes. Specifically, we found the following:

- Not all key strategies proposed were measurable;
- alignment between stated outcomes and reported measures was limited;
- operational measures of 'core deliverables and priorities' in these plans were underrepresented;
- strategic projects milestones were used as proxy measures in lieu of deliverable outcomes;
- operational impact of planned strategies was unaccounted in plans;
- key services were not clearly articulated and therefore not clearly measured. For example, the 'maintenance program completion' was identified as measure, clearly not reflecting an outcome (e.g. improved road and traffic conditions) but rather an action (i.e. completion of maintenance tasks);
- key financial and customer satisfaction outcome measures were either omitted or reported separately thus missing the opportunity to create the strategic linkages between financial and customer outcomes;
- operational measures and indicators were used interchangeably; for example, call centre response times, social media followers along with library visitation and membership numbers are operational measures rather than strategic outcome measures;
- operational measures were used in an ad-hoc manner as proxies for outcome indicators.

The outcome of this analysis identified key areas of work to further integrate operational and strategic performance measurement and management. While some measures and indicators were robust, others needed further development. Our approach to improving certain measures was to identify existing organisational sources which could be used. For example, the organisation invested heavily in a bi-annual customer survey, however it did not translate the findings from the survey into operational actions or performance measures and targets. This provided an opportunity for:

- Integration of satisfaction criteria from the survey as part of the suite of customer outcome indicators and measure;
- redefining the content of the survey and reporting frequency to better align with the strategic outcomes and reporting cycles.

The *financial resourcing* strategy and the associated financial measure were robust and well established. Interestingly these were not strongly integrated as part of the strategic objectives and outcomes. Yet, the resourcing strategy was a key driver to determine which programs and projects the organisation could afford to fund in the medium and short term. Similarly, the organisation had also developed *asset resourcing* and *workforce resourcing strategies* which included some robust analysis and measures. However, there was a lack of integration between these and the medium and short-term plans and performance reports. Furthermore, operationally the organisation was a service provider, however the scope of service provision was not recognised as a strategic outcome.

The lack of integration between various strategic outcomes was recognised by the organisation as influencing priority settings and diluting the achievement of such outcomes. Furthermore, strategic outcomes were not prioritised with full consideration of the impact on necessary asset resourcing and workforce capacity. This observation triggered a deeper review of organisational strategy and associated measures. It soon became clear that the strategic objectives and outcome indicators in their current form were not fully supporting meaningful measures for operational integration.

Though it was recognised by the organisation that further work on the articulation of the strategic priorities and outcomes was necessary, *Municipal* considered this as a subsequent phase in development and implementation of the performance measurement and management framework. We therefore supported *Municipal* in commencing the development of the performance measurement framework via the operations activities and measures element discussed above. The analysis of the operations and the identification of measures would

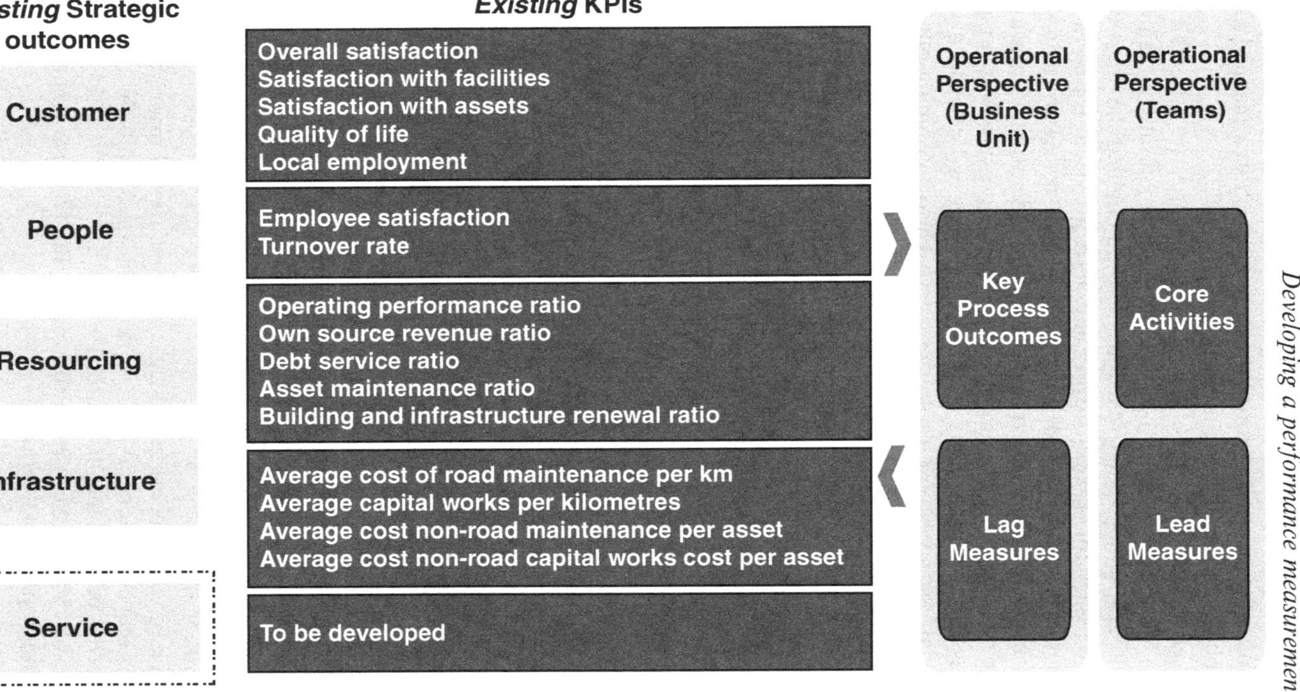

Figure 5.3 PMM framework linking existing strategic outcomes and KPI measures.

then inform the strategic prioritisation work which was planned as a second phase and part of the annual planning cycle.

Through the development of operational measures, we were able to 'zoom-in' and understand the work of the organisation, gaining insights about the work that was done. This highlighted the 'must-do-work', necessary for service delivery and asset provision for community functioning, but was not strongly captured or acknowledge in existing measures. Insights from developing operational measures further demonstrate any tenuous linkages between expected strategic outcomes and the operations of *Municipal*. Once we developed the operational measures, we took the approach of Zooming-out to integrating short- and medium-term planning, with strategic and operational performance measures.

Building engagement with the PMM framework: Management interviews and workshop

We adopted a 'zoom-in, zoom-out' approach by drawing on the methodological tools of (Nicolini, 2009) to engage with *Municipal* work by considering both operational and strategic activities. The aim was to develop a complete understanding of existing organisational practice, challenges and experiences to ascertain the level of competence with respect to performance measurement and management. It encompassed interviews with managers and some team leaders to understand the scope of their accountabilities and how existing performance measures informed their operational decisions. The interviews also served as a key mechanism to gain insight into the degree to which performance measurement was embedded as an organisational practice. It was consistently recognised by those interviewed that within the current organisational approach to performance measurement and management there was:

- Limited connection between the strategic plan objectives and operational work;
- a lack of clarity between strategic and operational priorities;
- underrepresentation of core work of business units in existing reported performance measures;
- need to create a mechanism for voicing the resource demands of existing operational work.

Following the interviews, we conducted a 'managers workshop'. The managers workshop focused on three objectives. First to provide managers with an overview of the findings from our initial organisational analysis and interviews. Second to educate the managers on the resultant PMM conceptual Framework and implementation methodology. Third to agree on the purpose, design and deliverables from the team-based workshops.

Zooming-in developing operational performance measures: Team-based workshops

The PMM framework we deployed emphasises the multiple connections: among strategic outcomes; between strategic outcomes and operational activities; and between different operational activities (Micheli & Mari, 2014; Poister, 2010; Melnyk, et al., 2005). This is because the achievement of strategic outcomes is underpinned by the operations of the organisation; in other words, its key processes are achieved through core activities and jobs and relationships among them. It is therefore essential that, as part of developing operational measures, the key organisational processes and core activities are unpacked to surface:

- What is done and how it is done;
- what impact such doings have towards the delivery of outcomes;
- whether what is delivered is of a standard that creates community value whilst maintaining financial sustainability.

The team-based workshops were designed not only to educate team leaders and coordinators in the PMM Framework but also define and document key processes and associated core activities for each business unit. This initial work formed the foundation for the development of operational performance measures. By engaging directly with business unit managers and team leaders about their work, we were able to uncover *core deliverables and priorities* and a clear articulation of actual work done which was reported as often said to be invisible in legacy reporting structures. An example of this is that the use of contractors appears to be a key organisational practice. Whilst this approach is commonplace in many organisations to address resourcing gaps, significant work is required in sourcing, monitoring and contractors to ensure agreed service levels are met. It was interesting to note that work associated with contractors was not adequately captured as a key area of work for *Municipal* business units.

Capturing the measures via the lens of work and workflow also enabled the identification of the interrelationships that exist between business units in the co-production of *Municipal* customer-facing service for the community. Understanding and articulating the actual work done sustains attention on resource demands and capacity to go beyond core deliverables and priorities. Building on these understandings, we worked on developing meaningful, grounded and pragmatic measures for each business unit that represented 'core deliverables and priorities' – the ***must do*** work of *Municipal*. These measures were then collated to produce the catalogue of operational measures (lag and lead) to inform the development of ongoing actionable reporting for each business unit. The measures were designed to inform:

- Operational capacity captured in key processes and lag measures[1];
- core activities performance captured in lead measures[2];
- managerial decision and levers to manage ongoing performance.

We developed both lag measures for key processes and lead measures for core activities. Lag measures show whether performance has been achieved towards a target of a key process. Lead measures show whether performance is on track towards a target.

Figure 5.4 below shows the relationship between the strategic perspective, outcomes and KPIs (shown in detail in Figure 5.3 above) and common business unit lag measures, those common across many business units of *Municipal*. Also shown are unit-specific *key process lag measure,* for example, *Environment and Health Service* is the key process of the Compliance business.

After developing lag measures for the key processes of each team, we worked to develop a suite of lead measures linked to core activities. The purpose of lead measures is to show whether the performance of an activity is on track towards the achievement of a key process outcome. Lead measures also provide early warning signs of underperforming activities and are used to inform whether any intervention in key processes and activities is necessary. Figure 5.5 captures the conceptual relationship between lead to lag measures and between key process, core activities and jobs within operational units.

At the completion of the Team-based Workshops phase, the outputs from each workshop were captured and reported in a measurement catalogue. The measurement catalogue captured 'core deliverables and priorities' and set the foundation for identifying resource capacity to achieve further ongoing priorities. To sustain common organisational understandings about the PMM framework, and consistency in the use

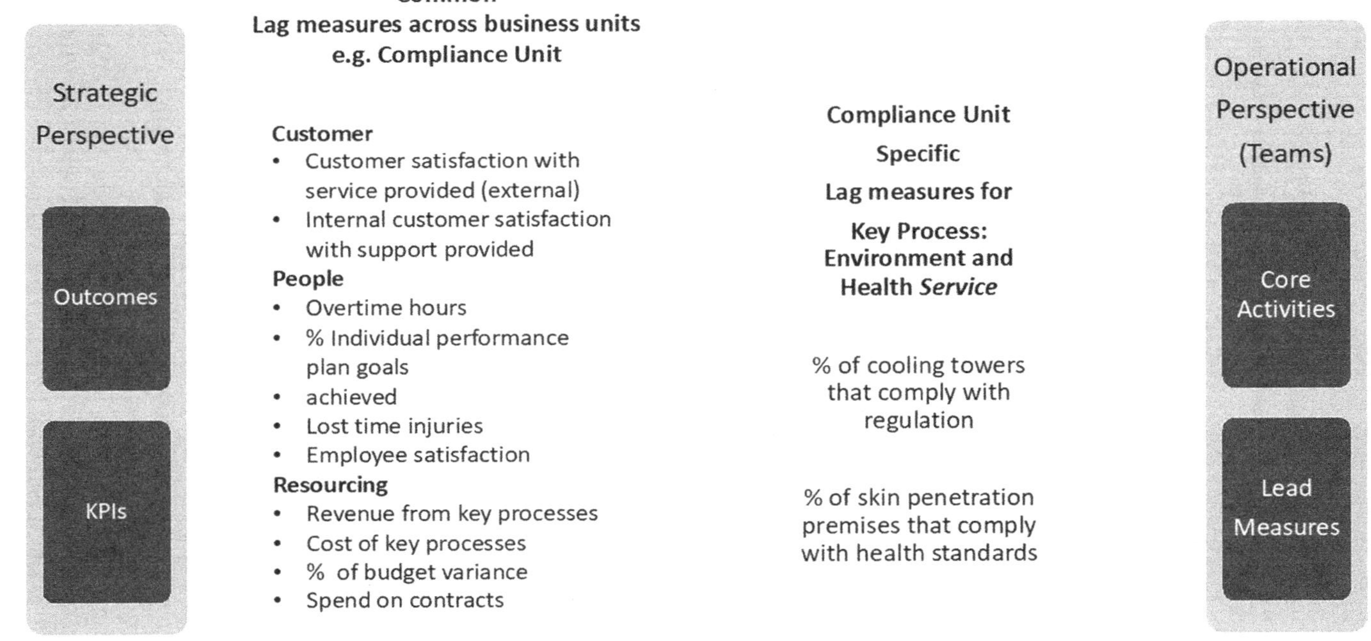

Figure 5.4 PMM framework compliance business unit lag measures for key process environment and health.

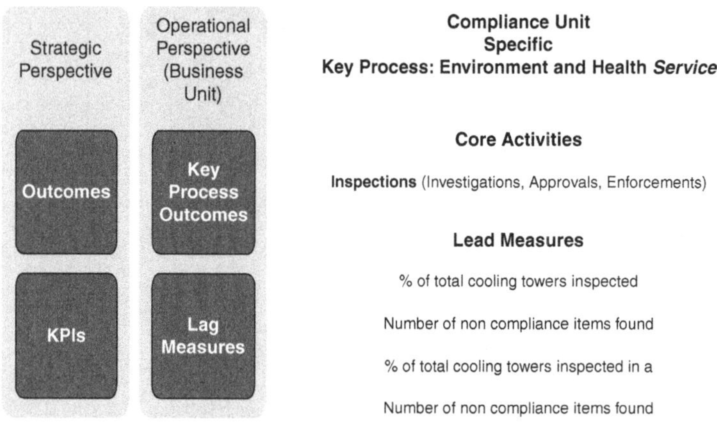

Figure 5.5 PMM framework compliance business unit key process and lead measures for core activities.

of different kinds of measures we included the following information in the measurement catalogue:

- Definitions of terms;
- operational unit responsibility;
- operational Unit Specific Lag (outcome) Measures;
- operational Unit Specific Lead Measures;
- key processes of business unit;
- activities for each key process;
- formulae for the calculation of measures;
- suggested frequency of reporting;
- manager responsible.

A simple spreadsheet was chosen to capture the catalogue. This was an intentional decision because this was the most accessible and used form of technology within this organisation and widely used across many organisations in this sector. We consciously made the decision not to distract managers with complicated 'dashboard' technologies or visuals. We firmly believe that such technology decisions can only be effectively made once the foundational work of identifying, defining and prioritising useful measures is complete.

The strategic outcome and KPIs were linked to the operational measures catalogue to enhance the connection between the strategic plan objectives and operational work. This addressed a key area of improvement identified by managers. Furthermore, the catalogue accommodates the recording of targets for each measure once operational measures are embedded in the organisational reporting cycle and baseline data is captured and analysed. Articulated in this way, meaningful measures can then be directly linked to and reported against specific strategies and outcomes which *Municipal* aspires to achieve. Table 5.1 *Snap-shot of PMM catalogue showing business unit lag and lead Measures* shows an example of the measurement catalogue items for the Compliance Unit.

Following the development of the measurement catalogue, a cycle of validation was undertaken. Managers and Team Leaders were given the opportunity to review the catalogue with the purpose of distilling the identified measures into a manageable reporting set. We asked managers to confirm:

- All activities were represented;
- most appropriate lead indicators were identified for each core process;
- most appropriate lag indicators were identified for each core process and resulting service;
- add any missing lead or lag measures.

In practice an important consideration for managers was the trade-off between the burden of collating and reporting data for the selected measures and the benefit that such performance information would bring to business unit operations and service delivery.

Zooming-out: Linking strategic outcomes and operations

The process of integrating short and medium-term planning with strategic and operational performance measures is a critical step in alignment of a PMM framework and the processes of planning and reporting. We achieved this by:

- Interconnecting different levels of measurement (i.e. operational lead and lag measures and strategic outcome KPIs);
- showing the relationship between levels of work (i.e. key processes, core activities and operational measures and strategic outcomes).

As shown in Figure 5.2 PMM Framework linking existing strategic outcomes and KPI measures, the strategic outcome indicators seek to bring together four interrelated outcome areas: Community,

Table 5.1 Snap-shot of PMM catalogue showing business unit lag and lead measures

Strategic outcome	*Business unit*	*Key process*	*Lag measure*	*Activities*	*Lead measure*	*Calculation*	*Unit of measure*	*Frequency*	*Manager responsible*
Auditing, Monitoring & Enforcement	Compliance	Environment & Health	% of cooling towers that comply with regulation	Inspections Investigations Approvals Enforcements	Cooling tower Inspections	Cooling tower Inspections/ Total Number	Percentage	Quarterly	Manager Compliance Team Leaders
	Compliance	Environment & Health	% of skin penetration premises that comply with health standards	Inspections Investigations Approvals Enforcements	Skin penetration premises	Skin penetration premises/ Total Number	Percentage	Quarterly	Manager Compliance Team Leaders

Infrastructure, were identified as the customer-facing outcomes which are supported by Financial Resources and People outcomes. Together these represent key strategic levers.

- *Community* as an outcome represents the organisations' role in creating and sustaining local communities. This is achieved by the organisation through its work in local governance, creation of place through long-term land use planning, promotion of economic development and lifestyles.
- *Infrastructure* as an outcome represents the organisation's work in the custodianship of public infrastructure (e.g. roads, parks and community building, bushland).

Underpinning the customer-facing outcomes of *Community* and *Infrastructure* are the *Financial Resources* and *People.* outcomes are subordinate outcomes and may be considered as enabling factors. *Financial Resources* outcomes determine the level of services provided and the kind and quality of assets that can be sustained. Furthermore, *Financial Resources* outcomes are important because as a public entity, using public money, the organisation must be accountable for using its financial resources responsibly and for the public good. The *People* outcomes are also a key factor, particularly in the service and asset provision work of *Municipal.* The investment and support of people are not only critical in a service-driven organisation but also one which relies on professional expertise in the development and sustainability of millions of dollars in public infrastructure investment.

Having identified the organisational strategic outcomes, consideration was given to how performance against such outcomes was to be measured. Performance at the outcome level is informed by high-level indicators sometimes referred to as key performance indicators. We maintain that key performance indicators (KPIs), as the name suggests, are only indications, representations or proxies for an outcome that is often not measurable, or unmeasurable by a single metric. It is not uncommon for KPIs to be represented by a collection or sets of measures that are indicative or relatable to the outcome or an aspect of an outcome being considered. KPIs are used to signal whether an outcome may be on track or may be achieved. We identified a number of meaningful measures to form KPIs that aligned with each of the strategic outcomes discussed above.

In addition to the already identified *Community* and *Infrastructure* outcomes and indicators and the associated subordinate *Financial Resources and People* outcomes as enabling factors, we identified that a core and missing strategic priority was *Service-associated* outcomes. In a public sector organisation, like *Municipal*, involved in the delivery of services to the community, service must be reflected a strategic outcome. We represented this in the dotted line box in Figure 5.3 above, as it was not yet explicitly identified and articulated as such by the organisation. We proposed the following definitional aspects:

- *Service* as an outcome represents organisational work in delivering numerous services to the local community (i.e. community development, childcare, libraries, events).

Service as an outcome must be reflected in the overarching performance measurement framework to reinforces the work of the organisation in service delivery but also the relationship between service delivery and the provision of infrastructure. A service view enables a clear line of sight, linking strategic outcomes (community and infrastructure) as well as various operational activities and measures. *Municipal*, had commenced some foundational work towards the development of an organisational service view, through the naming and identification of various services provided to the community. It had also completed two service reviews and profiles. Detailed work in developing a comprehensive organisational service view was beyond the scope of this project. It soon became clear that operationalising a service view and service profiles was difficult without an understanding of existing operational performance and strategic priorities. Therefore, a decision was made to focus on developing operational performance measures to understand existing operational capacity. To support this future imperative, we designed the performance measurement framework to include a strong emphasis on services (i.e. Service as a key outcome area) which could be populated with relevant service outcome indicators and measures once developed. Operational information could then be used to inform further activities aimed at the development of a service view for the organisation that included service profiles.

Future and further development of the PMM framework

At first, the catalogue may seem overwhelming in terms of scope. However, it was critical that upon the competition of the first iteration of PMM framework, Managers and the Executive Team were asked to work through and prioritise which measures were most relevant in terms of providing insights into:

- Performance in each Key Processes (and by association subordinate core activities);
- resource capability within each area of work;
- existing resource capacity to go beyond core work;
- which core work may require redefining.

This provided an opportunity for managers and their executives to have a deep discussion about performance measurement and what was key for their division and overall organisation. Furthermore, undertaking this work provided an opportunity for a realistic framing for the prioritisation of future strategies and outcomes as outlined in organisational strategic and operational plans.

The final step in the initial implementation process of the PMM framework involved embedding the operational measures in the organisational reporting cycle. This step then initiated the process of populating the new measures with data for analysis and establishment of performance baselines. Once performance baselines are established a process of further evaluation can commence. The efficacy of certain measures will then become clear as some measures will be retained, some will be modified, and others will be removed. This process of performance measurement review and refinement then becomes embedded in the organisational planning and performance framework with clear alignment to strategic priorities. Performance measurement and planning are ongoing, cyclical and emerging organisational work: as priorities change so should their measurement and thus establishing the foundation of robust organisational continuous improvement practice.

Future and further work recommended for the organisation was the development of comprehensive *Service* outcomes and attendant KPIs. The inclusion of service outcomes and KPIs would reflect the extensive service delivery work that the organisation undertakes. This could be achieved through:

- Defining community-facing services and the value created;
- identifying cross-functional contributions to value creation;
- identifying attendant 'value streams';
- identifying and linking service key process, activities and lead and lag measures.

This new work can then be embedded in the PMM framework and measures catalogue of the organisation to inform the performance of service delivery.

Concluding comments

As stated at the beginning of this chapter, an organisation may develop a performance management and measurement framework by commencing via any one of the three facets identified in Figure 5.1. This chapter captures the authors' experience in working in partnership with an organisation in the development of performance measurement capabilities. The case study details the processes and outcomes of the development of the PMM framework, rationale for adopting an initial operational measurement focus and the outcomes of this process. At the time of writing, the partner organisation was consolidating the performance measurement framework through the collection of baseline data to crystalise measures and provide insights into the usability of selected measures. The authors continue to support and advise the organisation through this process which will next focus on developing service outcomes and strategic priorities. The completion of these two elements will further sustain a strategic planning practice that draws upon stakeholder and operational input.

In concluding this chapter, we wish to share key learnings that have surfaced in this work. When commencing the development of a performance measurement and management framework, understanding the organisational context is essential. Taking time to engage in discussions with senior managers, managers and their teams is critical to understand their expectations, experiences and challenges, and the organisation approach to measurement. Analysing organisational documents, understanding the language used surrounding performance, measurement and planning is essential to ensure shared meanings and lexicon. These multiple touchpoint activities necessitate a level of flexibility to allow a zooming-in and zooming-out approach which is essential in developing insights and building engagement capital. Engagement capital works to inform subsequent activities and enables these to be adapted in context and in response to diverse levels of readiness, bits of knowledge and understandings of those involved.

Notes

1 **Lag/Outcome measure**: It is which informs whether the organisational or operational goal has been achieved.
2 **Lead/Driver measure:** It is which informs whether the organisation or operation is on track towards achieving a goal.

References

Andrews, R. and Van de Walle, S. 2013. New public management and citizens' perceptions of local service efficiency, responsiveness, equity and effectiveness. *Public Management Review*, *15*(5), pp. 762–783. https://doi.org/10.1080/14719037.2012.725757

Baird, K., Schoch, H. and Chen, Q.J. 2012. Performance management system effectiveness in Australian local government. *Pacific Accounting Review*, 24(2), pp. 161–185. https://doi.org/10.1108/01140581211258461

Boston, J. and Pallot, J. 1997. Linking strategy and performance: Developments in the New Zealand public sector. *Journal of Policy Analysis and Management: The Journal of the Association for Public Policy Analysis and Management*, *16*(3), pp. 382–404. https://doi.org/10.1002/1520-6688(199722)16:3%3C382::AID-PAM18%3E3.0.CO;2-S

Dollery, B., Grant, B. and Kortt, M. 2013. An evaluation of amalgamation and financial viability in Australian local government. *Public Finance & Management*, *13*(3), pp. 215–238.

Greater Sydney Commission (n.d.). *The Greater Western Sydney Commission Plan (2018) A Metropolis of Three Cities— The Greater Sydney Region Plan*, available at: https://www.greater.sydney/metropolis-of-three-cities (accessed 3 November 2019).

Johnsson, M.C., Pepper, M., Price, O.M. and Richardson, L.P. 2021. "Measuring up": a systematic literature review of performance measurement in Australia and New Zealand local government. *Qualitative Research in Accounting & Management*, *18*(2), pp. 195–227. https://doi.org/10.1108/QRAM-11-2020-0184

Joshi, M.P., Kathuria, R. and Porth, S.J. 2003. Alignment of strategic priorities and performance: An integration of operations and strategic management perspectives. *Journal of Operations Management*, *21*(3), pp. 353–369. https://doi.org/10.1016/S0272-6963(03)00003-2

Melnyk, S.A., Calantone, R.J., Luft, J., Stewart, D.M., Zsidisin, G.A., Hanson, J. and Burns, L. 2005. An empirical investigation of the metrics alignment process. *International Journal of Productivity and Performance Management*, 54 (5/6), pp. 312–324. https://doi.org/10.1108/17410400510604494

Micheli, P. and Mari, L. 2014. The theory and practice of performance measurement. *Management accounting research*, *25*(2), pp. 147–156. https://doi.org/10.1016/j.mar.2013.07.005

Nath, D. and Sudharshan, D. 1994. Measuring strategy coherence through patterns of strategic choices. *Strategic Management Journal*, *15*(1), pp. 43–61. https://doi.org/10.1002/smj.4250150104

Nicolini, D. 2009. Zooming in and out: Studying practices by switching theoretical lenses and trailing connections. *Organization Studies*, *30*(12), pp. 1391–1418. https://doi.org/10.1177/0170840609349875

NSW Office of Local Government 2020. Integrated planning and reporting, https://www.olg.nsw.gov.au/councils/integrated-planning-and-reporting/ (accessed 4 February 2020).

Poister, T.H. 2010. The future of strategic planning in the public sector: Linking strategic management and performance. *Public Administration Review*, *70*(s1), pp. 246–254. https://doi.org/10.1111/j.1540-6210.2010.02284.x

Pollitt, C. 2018. Performance management 40 years on: A review. Some key decisions and consequences. *Public Money & Management*, *38*(3), pp. 167–174. https://doi.org/10.1080/09540962.2017.1407129

6 Case study #3 Critical success factors

Introduction

Managers in public sector organisations often find the implementation of continuous improvement initiatives challenging. There are many interconnected factors that affect the successful implementation of these initiatives. There are also many actors or stakeholders who can play a part in this implementation journey because of their attitudes and interests towards these initiatives (Elias, 2008). This chapter therefore builds upon chapter two, which considered the landscape of continuous improvement by focusing on the identification of factors critical to success of continuous improvement initiatives. Therefore, the objective of this chapter is to present ten critical success factors identified from recent research conducted by the authors of this book. Findings from research with a selection of local and regional councils in Australia and New Zealand were used to distil critical success factors specifically focused on the experiences of these organisations. This chapter begins with a review of the literature and presents the critical success factors associated with continuous improvement in this literature. Second, this chapter introduces the research conducted in the Australia-New Zealand context which informed the distillation of critical factors into a top ten list. The concludes with a discussion of ten critical success factors that can help local councils in their continuous improvement journey. (A checklist for practitioners to use is presented in full in the appendix.)

Critical success factors in the continuous improvement literature

Academic literature on continuous improvement provides some definitions and explanations for the term critical success factors. For

DOI: 10.4324/9781003011675-6

example, Jeyaraman & Teo (2010) explored the concept of critical success factors and found that critical success factors are those few things that must go well to ensure success. In further distilling this definition, they also propose that critical success factors are the essential things that must be achieved by an organisation to identify which areas will deliver the greatest competitive leverages. The academic literature explains that critical success factors are not major objectives but rather are those actions and processes that can be controlled by the organisation to achieve its goals.

A review of the existing body of knowledge covering the concept of continuous improvement and critical success factors reveals two major issues. First, current literature stemming from research on continuous improvement is heavily skewed towards the private sector, with a lesser engagement with the public sector. Secondly, researchers in the field of continuous improvement have reported on their attempts to identify critical success factors. Examples from different countries and different contexts are available in the literature. However, there are few studies exploring critical success factors in the A & NZ context available in this literature.

In a review of literature, Fryer and her co-researchers in the United Kingdom conducted an analysis of existing literature that included critical success factors of continuous improvement in public sector organisations (Fryer, et al., 2007). They found 29 research articles that covered such critical success factors and based on their research they recommended 13 key critical success factors. These critical success factors are: management commitment, customer management, supplier management, quality data, measurement and reporting, teamwork, communication, process management, ongoing evaluation, monitoring and assessment, training and learning, employee empowerment, having aims and objectives that are communicated to the workforce and used to prioritise individual's actions – a corporate quality culture, production design and organisational structure.

In another research project, Gonzalez-Aleu and his co-researchers tried to identify critical success factors for continuous improvement in hospitals. Using a survey, they collected 116 responses from hospitals that were involved in at least one continuous improvement project during the previous two years. Their study came up with 53 critical success factors. They further classified these into five categories: critical success factors for task design category; critical success factors for team design category; critical success factors for organization category and critical success factors for continuous improvement project process category (Gonzalez Aleu & Van Aken, 2016).

In another related study, Youssef & Zairi (1995) analysed a list of 22 critical factors based on the Malcolm Baldrige National Quality Award. These factors included management commitment, customer satisfaction, clear mission statements, culture change, education, participative management, strategic quality plan, goal clarity, error prevention, top management steering committee, problem-solving, measurement, problem identification, goal setting, recognition programme, quality circles/improvement, vendor partnerships, project improvement procedure, publicised success, statistical process control, cost of quality and zero defect attitude. While benchmarking these 22 critical factors across countries (e.g. the United Kingdom, Middle East, Malaysia and Singapore) and industry sectors (e.g. Healthcare), they found that a few factors like clear commitment towards customer satisfaction, clear mission statement and top management commitment were critical across all organisations.

In yet another study, Antony and his co-researchers identified the critical success factors for continuous improvement in higher educational institutions. Their study focussed on lean six sigma as a continuous improvement approach. The critical success factors identified in their study are uncompromising top management support and commitment, effective communication at all levels vertically and horizontally, strategic and visionary leadership, developing organisational readiness, resources and skills to facilitate implementation, project selection and prioritisation and organisational culture (Antony, et al., 2012).

Comparing the different critical success factors identified in these studies highlight both similarities and differences. For example, leadership aspects like management commitment and cultural aspects like organisational culture were identified as common critical success factors in most of these studies. But these studies also differ in terms of context, type of public sector organisation and host country, resulting in the identification of different factors like quality data and error prevention.

Academic literature on continuous improvement includes other research studies that focus on critical success factors (e.g. Alhaqbani, 2017). However, not many of these research studies are about continuous improvement in public sector organisations and within those public sector studies, the literature is scant on local government. Furthermore, studies exploring Australia-New Zealand context is limited in the existing literature. Therefore, this chapter explores the Australia-New Zealand context by investigating the implementation of continuous improvement in selected local and regional councils in Australia and New Zealand.

Australia New Zealand context

The research project that formed the basis of this chapter aimed at identifying critical success factors for the successful implementation of continuous improvement projects in the Australia New Zealand context. For this purpose, local government organisations from Australia and New Zealand were selected for this project. As the specific focus was on local government organisations, this project included one regional council and three local councils in the Wellington region of New Zealand and a group of continuous improvement practitioners working in local government in the Australian State of NSW.

Each of the councils and the group of practitioners selected for this study was involved in at least one continuous improvement project during the past three years. Data collection about these projects was conducted using structured interviews with selected stakeholders. For the NZ data collection, a total of 17 interviews were conducted with internal stakeholders: senior managers, middle-level officers in charge of the continuous improvement project and other council staff members as well as suppliers and ratepayers of the council. The Australian data collection involved a focus group with seven continuous improvement professionals representing seven local government organisations.

As most of the existing literatures report on critical success factors derived from studies conducted outside Australia and New Zealand, special attention was given to the research discussed in the chapter on attempting to surface critical success factors relevant to the local context. Accordingly, data collection and analysis included comparing the critical success factors identified in this study with what is already available in the literature. Essentially these have been distilled to ten critical success factors identified in this chapter and discussed in the following section.

Ten critical success factors

i Top management commitment

Top management commitment is crucial for the successful implementation of continuous improvement projects. Commitment from the top management often requires the direct involvement of senior managers in continuous improvement projects. Communicating and encouraging staff to become involved in improvement projects and/or providing appropriate incentives to staff and others to remain engaged is an essential part of this commitment. This finding for A & NZ is in line with the findings of other studies that were conducted outside the Australia-New Zealand region discussed above.

In further unpacking of the nature of this CSF, two types of top management commitment were observed. The first type was a top-down approach in which the Chief Executive or a Senior Executive of the organisation was directly involved in initiating the continuous improvement project. In such cases, top management commitment came in the shape of owning the project and in some cases directing the staff to get involved in the project. The second type, was more of a bottom-up approach, when a staff member or a group of staff initiated the project and convinced a Chief Executive or a senior leader to want the project to progress beyond the initial scoping stages and brief. Although the level of commitment in this latter type was lower than the first, this research found that the success level of these projects was high.

The importance of top management commitment in a local council can be summarised using the following quotes. The first from a project-lead who participated in this study:

> *This project was started by our CE....before joining our council she had worked in private organisations.....she had successful experience in managing CI projects....she was the one who asked me to become the project lead...she was very confident about the usefulness of continuous improvement in an organisation...whenever I had tricky issues, I went to her......without her support we would have found it really difficult to implement the project as not everyone was originally supportive.*

Management commitment of the first type was also reflected in where the continuous improvement responsibilities are situated in the organisational hierarchy for example embedding such resources in '*in the general manager's office... Executive services specifically looking after the mayor and Councillors and then ultimately any escalated customer issues that go to the general manager, I pick up. I work with that perspective*' [CI Professional 1]. In contrast, the second type of commitment was demonstrated when the continuous improvement professional was able to understand the values and interests of the General Manager so that they were effective in '*linking* [the] *program to what your General Manager got excited about*' [CI Professional 2]

ii Middle management support and involvement

In addition to the top management commitment, middle management support and involvement are critical to the successful implementation of a continuous improvement project in a local council. While top management can provide the strategic direction of a continuous improvement initiative, the operational leadership and management of such projects are often provided by middle-level managers. It is important to note here that just their support may not be adequate for the effective implementation of a continuous improvement project, but in many cases their active involvement in the operations related to this project will decide the success of these projects.

Not all previous reports in the existing literature recognise middle management support and involvement as a critical success factor. However, in this study, it was found that even after receiving top management commitment, some of the projects became slow and struggled in its implementation due to a lack of middle management involvement. It was interesting to note that most of the middle managers were not against the project as such, but they did not actively become involved in the project, resulting in low effectiveness at the operational level implementation of the project. The following quote by a local council staff member captures the essence of this critical success factor:

> *This project would have been much more successful if my manager was more involved in it.... he was not against it, but he was not engaged in it.... he did not discourage me, but he did not encourage me either.... he did not have time I think...the senior leadership of this council was much more interested compared to these guys.*

iii Project champion

Another critical factor in the success of a continuous improvement project in a local council is the presence and contributions of a project champion. A project champion is usually a middle-level manager, a project leader, or a non-managerial level staff member. At times even a senior leader in the organisation can take the role of a project champion. A successful project champion is totally committed to the project, gets involved in the project from its early stages, takes the role of a problem solver to solve any issues during the execution of the project, and provides leadership throughout the project till it is successfully completed.

Almost all the projects considered in this study had a project champion. In some projects, this role was taken by a project lead who was formally appointed with the intention of taking up the role of a project champion. This study also found a few instances when a team member in a continuous improvement project took up the role informally and worked hard for the successful execution of this project. In both cases, the passion and commitment of this person towards the project was a key ingredient to the success of the project. The following words of a chief executive in a local council provide a good description of a project champion:

> *I might have started this project, but without Matt (name disguised) we would not have reached this point.......he was totally committed, hardworking and when I recommended his name at the very start of this project, I knew that he will do a great job.....his passion is contagious and when people are tired he lifts up their morale.......there were times when we were not sure about proceeding with this project but he was determined.*

In contrast, Championing was also something that was discussed by the continuous improvement professionals. Championing in this case, however emerged from an ongoing passion for a tool that then became the sole focus, rather than being embedded as part of a broader and more strategic project initiative:

> *... it's a general managers passion and he was my director before he became a general manager and we always had to do it in our team... we mostly process map focus... It wasn't around the quality improvement, it was more about just mapping what you're doing so that you would easily ... someone else could do it*

When the nature of the project is not strategically linked or focussing on the customer, such championing may not be as effective and may detract from this factor being critical to success. The role of Project Championing is therefore critical in determining the strategic impact of projects.

iv Commitment to the indigenous community

In the New Zealand context, commitment and engagement of the local council with the indigenous community are critical to the success of a continuous improvement project. For example, in New Zealand, the

Local Government Act 2002 requires councils to consider and promote the current and future wellbeing of communities. This act also introduced new responsibilities and opportunities for engagement and cooperation between councils and Māori. So, while introducing continuous improvement initiatives, the project team should clearly understand how it will impact Iwi, Hapu and Māori groups and design appropriate engagement strategies with them.

Interestingly, the majority of the existing literature on continuous improvement that are mainly based on studies outside Australia and New Zealand, does not recognise the commitment to the indigenous community as a critical success factor. But the New Zealand context is different. In many local councils in this region, there are inbuilt organisational mechanisms to engage with the indigenous community. In fact, this study found that there is a high risk of failure if a continuous improvement goes ahead without consulting and engaging with the indigenous community. It is a part of the culture for most of the local councils in this region. The following words of a Chief Executive highlight this point:

> *Engagement with our Iwi is a no brainer...... all our projects start with the consultation and involvement of our local Iwi...they are the people of this land and it is our responsibility as a council to understand and promote their wellbeing....it is a part of our culture....we have council staff who are experienced and dedicated to involving with the indigenous community....we also celebrate the success of our projects with them.*

v ***Speed of project planning and execution***

The pace of project planning and execution in a public sector organisation can be often slower than a private sector organisation whose focus is on maximising profits. A public sector organisation has different constraints and purposes in comparison to a private sector organisation. The speed of project planning and execution is a critical success factor in the successful implementation of a continuous improvement in a local council. This does not necessarily mean that local councils must be slow in planning and executing a continuous improvement project, but they should adopt an appropriate pace within the constraints and culture of that local council.

Speed of project planning and execution does not appear as a critical success factor in most of the existing research publications on continuous improvement. But this study identified it as crucial in getting the support and involvement of the council staff who are involved in the project. Too much push from the top management or project champion may create opposition and confusion among project participants that may have negative impacts. In addition, a continuous improvement project initiated by a local council may affect stakeholders external to the council and it may take time to engage and convince them about the outcomes of the project. Therefore, project planning and execution must be done thoroughly at an appropriate pace. This critical success factor can be explained using a quote from a project lead:

> *We have to manage this journey properly, slowly and over time...... when we tried to push and run fast, it became slower....... we have to walk before we run...we also have to engage with our external stakeholders and that takes time.....we are not a private organisation...we have a commitment and responsibility to a wide variety of stakeholders....finally we are responsible to our local community....that old phrase is very true, slow and steady wins the race.*

vi Effective communication

Unsurprisingly, effective communication is vital for the successful implementation of continuous improvement projects in local councils. Interestingly, most of the research studies on continuous improvement identify effective communication as a critical success factor in private and public sector organisations. Effective communication involves timely, regular, clear messages about the continuous improvement project covering all levels of the organisation. It also includes communication with external stakeholders who are involved or affected by the continuous improvement project. Through effective communication, both internal and external stakeholders can become more engaged and can even work as a team for various problem-solving scenarios during the execution of the project.

In this study, lack of communication was found as a main contributing factor towards the failure of some continuous improvement projects. When negativity and confusion about the project are not addressed at the right time through proper communication, it can result in escalating situations with the potential to get out of hand and be difficult to control. When the project champion, project lead or even the CEO are actively involved in providing effective communication about the project, local councils can establish a common language for change and improvement, while realising continuous improvement initiatives. The following words of a team member from a continuous improvement project provides a good explanation of the need for effective communication:

> *This project would have yielded much better outcomes if we had better communication.....I think the main problem was that the communication was late.....people had become too negative about the what, why and how of this project...we really lacked a project champion who would provide timely communication about this project.*

Similarly, communication and specifically, honesty as a feature of communication was identified as critical in explaining the purpose of the continuous improvement work. This was highlighted by CI Practitioner 2 who suggested that it was critical to be '*honest when ... communicating to other people about what the why is. I think that's really important....be really smart about how you communicate with other people, especially your general manager'*. This was found to be a view shared among the Australian continuous improvement practitioners.

vii Organisational culture

The organisational culture in the local council is a critical factor that can determine the success of a continuous improvement project. Existing literature on continuous improvement has recognised this factor but uses different terms like organisational culture, organisational readiness, culture change, corporate quality culture etc. In essence, the shared values, beliefs, and assumptions of the organisational need to be conducive for the implementation of a continuous improvement project.

The local councils that participated in this study were comparatively large organisations. Many of these councils consist of different units like facilities management, infrastructure, leadership, finance, strategic planning, communications, and human resources. This study found that 'silo thinking' was an acute issue among some of the units within a local council. As continuous improvement projects tend to cut across different organisational units, its success was dependant on the cooperation between these units and their ability to work together as a team. In this context, it is critical to have an organisational culture that supports cooperation, teamwork, and innovation. The criticality of organisational culture can be captured using the words of a project lead in one of the continuous improvement projects:

> *There is a lot of silo thinking in our council…. 'me thing' is also not uncommon among some of the participants in these projects…our organisational culture has to change if we are serious about achieving positive results from these projects…we should learn how to work together as a team…otherwise this is a waste of time.*

viii Project selection

Selecting the right project at the right time during the continuous improvement journey is critical for a local government organisation. Reports in the existing literature warn about the risks associated with wrong project selection resulting in frustration, delay, and demotivation. So, selecting projects that have a direct impact on the organisation's mission and strategy, that can be completed on time are important. These provide success stories showing measurable improvements which can then be used to further the momentum of continuous improvement in the organisation.

In this study, those local councils who excelled in project selection started with easy projects or low-hanging fruits. Their experiences with low-hanging fruits helped them to tackle difficult projects at a later stage in their continuous improvement journey. The following quote of the senior manager captures this factor:

> *Our strategy was to start with the easy projects, those low hanging fruits…. we used them as success stories to get the buy in from our stakeholders…. later we selected more difficult projects.*

ix Adequate resources

For any continuous improvement initiative to be successful, it is critical for the organisation to support it by providing adequate financial and personnel resources. In the case of local government, resources may include time, money, people and technology. Adequate resources are not an exclusive critical success factor for local councils, as existing studies have already highlighted adequate resources as critical for the success of continuous improvement projects in both public and private sector organisations.

In this study, successful continuous improvement projects budgeted an appropriate amount of money for the implementation of these projects. When required, project team members were released from or allowed reduced workload in their routine jobs to engage in these projects. Additionally, the project team members were provided training on tools related to continuous improvement, project management and change management. The following words of project team member highlight the criticality of this factor:

> *Our project was successful because the senior management committed resources for it…they understood that it takes time out of our regular jobs…. training on lean, statistical process and project management was really useful for all of us.*

x Inclusive stakeholder management

Understanding and managing stakeholders are critical for the success of continuous improvement projects. As a critical success factor, stakeholder management plays an important role in local government organisations, particularly due to their key role in representing and servicing community needs. Inclusively identify stakeholders who can affect or are affected by a continuous improvement project is therefore essential in project success. Inclusive stakeholder management would also include efficient processes and effective negotiations while engaging with the project stakeholders. This aspect of stakeholder management will be discussed in greater detail in Chapter 4 of this book.

The existing literature on continuous improvement does not usually list stakeholder management as a critical success factor. But in this study, an inclusive identification and management of stakeholders, that is, not just customers or community or a few groups as the stakeholders, but considering all groups or individuals who can affect or is affected by the project was seen as a critical success factor. The following words of a project lead capture the criticality of stakeholder management:

> *One great learning from this project was to understand that our stakeholders are not just council members, customers or even our community……they are much more than that….we learned that a local council have a multitude of stakeholders…and we don't know who will become the key and when…we have to be inclusive.*

Conclusions

This chapter highlighted ten critical factors for the successful implementation of a continuous improvement project in a local council. These critical success factors are top management commitment, middle management support and involvement, project champion, commitment to the indigenous community, speed of project planning and execution, effective communication, organisational culture, project selection, adequate resources, and inclusive stakeholder management. Some of these factors were already identified in the existing literature (e.g. top commitment) while some new critical success factors emerged out of this study that focussed on the Australia New Zealand context (e.g. commitment to the indigenous community). In the post-Covid-19 world, it is important that CI practitioners adapt these factors innovatively (Elias, 2021).

Overall, this chapter contributes a set of critical success factors to the existing literature on continuous improvement in the public sector (e.g. Elias & Davis, 2018). With a specific focus on local councils, this chapter also plugs a gap in the existing literature by providing a study that explores the Australia-New Zealand context. Finally, a checklist is provided in Appendix 1 for those practitioners who are preparing for a continuous improvement journey in a local government setting. It is recommended that they modify it by fitting it for their purpose and context.

References

Alhaqbani, A.M. 2017. *Continuous improvement: Critical success factors in the Saudi public service sector*, Doctoral dissertation, University of Portsmouth.

Antony, J., Krishan, N., Cullen, D. and Kumar, M. 2012. Lean Six Sigma for higher education institutions (HEIs): Challenges, barriers, success factors, tools/techniques. *International Journal of Productivity and Performance Management*, *61*(8), pp. 940–948. https://doi.org/10.1108/17410401211277165

Elias, A.A. 2008. Group model building: Energy efficiency in New Zealand's residential sector. Proceedings of the*6th Annual Australian and New Zealand Academy of Management Operations Management Symposium*, Gold Coast, Australia.

Elias, A.A. and Davis, D. 2018. Analysing public sector continuous improvement: A structures approach. *International Journal of Public Sector Management*, *31*(1), pp. 2–13. https://doi.org/10.1108/IJPSM-08-2016-0135

Elias, A.A. 2021. Kerala's innovations and flexibility for Covid-19 recovery: Storytelling using systems thinking. *Global Journal of Flexible Systems Management*, 22 (1), pp. 33-43.https://doi.org/10.1007/s40171-021-00268-8.

Fryer, K.J., Antony, J. and Douglas, A. 2007. Critical success factors of continuous improvement in the public sector: A literature review and some key findings. *The TQM Magazine*, *19*(5), pp. 497–517. https://doi.org/10.1108/09544780710817900

Gonzalez Aleu, F. and Van Aken, E.M. 2016. Systematic literature review of critical success factors for continuous improvement projects. *International Journal of Lean Six Sigma*, *7*(3), pp. 214–232. https://doi.org/10.1108/IJLSS-06-2015-0025

Jeyaraman, K. and Teo, L.K. 2010. A conceptual framework for critical success factors of lean Six Sigma Implementation on the performance of electronic manufacturing service industry. *Journal of Lean Six Sigma Lean Six Sigma implementation*, *1*(3), pp. 191–215. https://doi.org/10.1108/20401461011075008

Youssef, M.A. and Zairi, M. 1995. Benchmarking critical factors for TQM: Part II – empirical results from different regions in the world. *Benchmarking for Quality Management & Technology*, *2*(2), pp. 3–19. https://doi.org/10.1108/14635779510090517

7 Case study #4—Understanding the work of CI practitioners

A case study from NSW, Australia

Local government organisations in Australia have invested in the implementation of various quality and CI programs for over two decades, and some (e.g. Wollongong City Council and Bankstown City Council, which are now amalgamated as Canterbury-Bankstown Council), have done so since the 1990s. In fact, various local government organisations were so deeply invested in the implementation of CI that they participated in the industry-wide calibration of their quality efforts via the Australia Business Excellence awards process. Recipients of this national award (between 1995 and 2017) include:

- Wollongong City Council;
- Bankstown City Council (now Canterbury-Bankstown Council);
- Baulkham Hills Shire (NSW);
- Hobart City Council (TAS);
- City of Wodonga (Vic);
- The City of Nedlands (WA);
- City of Marion (SA);
- City of Joondalup (WA).

Drawing on this strong industry investment, it was time to consider more deeply the work of CI practitioners that have been contributing to the sustainability of CI in the local government sector. A survey was conducted by the authors with a community of CI practitioners working in local government across the State of New South Wales, Australia. Though the practitioners held various roles in their respective organisations, a major part of each of their roles was focused on CI. The practitioners came together as a community of practice to discuss their CI work, challenges and experiences. The purpose of the

DOI: 10.4324/9781003011675-7

community of practice was to share ideas, help and support each other via collaboration and education. The survey of approximately 20 members of this community of practice was the first step in a mixed-methods research project, where practitioners then participated in a focus group and some participated in follow-up interviews.

Models in use

The findings of this research suggest that various quality models were adopted by respondents. On the basis of the models adopted, varying continuous improvement approaches and tools were implemented. Although the ABEF had a significant presence in local government for some time, other frames were also being adopted. These are shown in Figure 7.1.

The findings showed that while 24% of practitioners reported using the ABEF, other approaches such as Lean were also reported by 38% of practitioners and Lean Six Sigma by 20% of practitioners. Interestingly, only 5% of respondents reported utilising ISO standards, which had been a popular framework of choice in the early years of CI in local government, when organisations were responding to the State-driven competitive tendering policies.

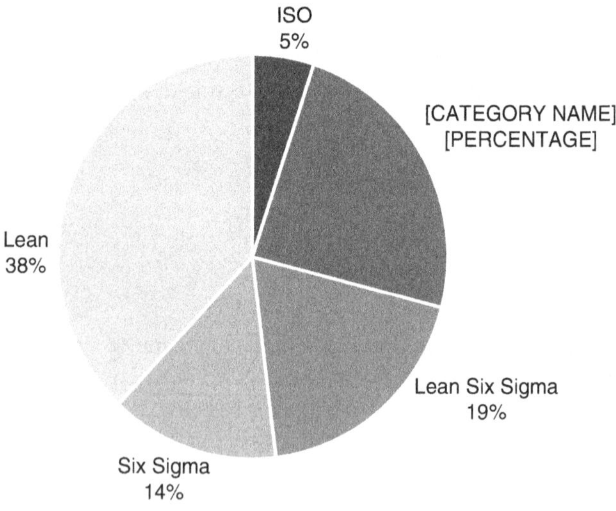

Figure 7.1 Models of quality in use.

Diversity of accountability and responsibility for CI

Accountability and responsibility for CI can sit in various different departments within any organisation and this is, of course, no different for local government. Findings from the survey supported this perspective. Respondents of the survey reported that CI responsibilities were part of various departments including:

- IT and Business Transformation
- Customer Services
- People and Culture
- People and Strategy
- Finance and Corporate Performance
- Governance and Engagement

The findings also revealed that in addition to the diversity of departmental responsibility and reporting lines also existed. Some CI practitioners reported directly to senior executives, while others reported to middle or functional managers (e.g. Customer Service Manager vs Corporate Services Director). The structuring of the CI accountability was also found to be diverse, often as a result of organisational resource investment for such programs. In some instances, CI expertise was centralised in a discrete department which worked across the organisation with different functional areas to implement the CI program. In other instances, CI practitioners were part of operational teams focusing on the implementation of CI within their work area or the centralised team provided support to CI practitioners in the operations.

This diversity highlights that CI implementation can take a centralised, decentralised or hybrid form. The size of centralised teams was on average 3–4 team members including a coordinator; in hybrid models, a centralised team supported on average between 8 and 12 specialists who reported to various managers dispersed across the organisation. In decentralised models, the approach to CI was less consistent and was more strongly aligned with the preferences of the manager responsible. The larger organisations (i.e. between 1000 and 1300 employees) tended to have larger decentralised teams, while smaller organisations (i.e. 320–500 employees) not unexpectedly have smaller teams dedicated to CI or decentralised teams focused on specific areas of business (e.g. customer service). The various resource investments in CI, the implementation form (i.e. centralised, decentralised or hybrid) as well as the functional location of CI practitioners also give rise to diversity in the ways in which CI implementations were characterised – the frameworks adopted, the manner of implementation and emphasis given to CI work. These aspects were articulated by a CI practitioner from the Australian State of NSW during a research interview. When asked about the decision of where to appoint accountability and responsibility for continuous improvement the practitioner responded:

> *...Ultimately it depends on what services are being offered within BI [Business Improvement was used in this organisation to refer to continuous improvement]. An organisational approach needs the appropriate centralised resources to drive this as it is too big for any one or two FTE to do alone. So depending on the actual business Improvement services and scale it would best sit within a BT to Corporate team. However, if you're just looking for efficiencies and gradual improvements then an independent Corporate team with a decentralised approach (in partnership with Managers) would be sufficient.*

In the more strategic areas, for example when CI practitioners were part of departments such as People and Culture or People and Strategy, there seemed to be greater consideration given to the broader implications of CI for organisational policy, people and strategy outcomes. The approach to CI involved strategic service reviews, development of performance measurement and management frameworks, workforce development and engagement initiatives to facilitate broader organisational change. CI in these contexts was understood to be about '*organisational development [and] capability development* and ideally reporting '*straight to* [the] *CEO'* (CI Practitioner in People & Culture Unit from the Australian State of NSW).

In contrast, CI practitioners in operational areas had a greater emphasis on process and workflow improvement at the grassroots level, including the implementation of new technology. As a CI practitioner working within an operational unit explained when CI was implemented in her area:

> .. using things like PDCA, we were process mapping, we were looking at root-cause analysis. So really just kind of identifying the things that we were doing really well, and then those other opportunities for improvement.

These practitioners engaged in process mapping and procedure documentation and relying on it as a key tool to initiate efficiency, effectiveness and standardisation of processes which at times supported the introduction of new technologies.

Activities undertaken by CI practitioners in local government

CI practitioners reported engaging in various methodologies and tools to drive CI within their organisations. Commonly adopted methodologies included the Deming Cycle (Plan Do Check Act or PDCA), DMAIC framework (Define, Measure, Analyse, Improve and Control) and the ABEF ADRI Cycle. When CI practitioners were asked what activities dominated their time in realising each stage of their chosen methodology, some interesting activity profiles emerged. Figure 7.2 shows the percentage of survey respondents for each reported activity.

Recording what is done in existing processes is reported as a key activity within 66% of respondents. This recording of existing processes almost exclusively took the form of process mapping and/or developing written procedures. About 57% of respondents reported engaging in business improvement project facilitation or leadership. While 48% of respondents reported engaging in training of employees in CI tools. Surprisingly, though all respondents reported adopting a CI methodology which includes a significant component of measurement and analysis, only 33% of CI practitioners reported engaging in performance measurement and data analysis as a core activity. Similarly, only 33% reported engaging in organisational change activities at a strategic level.

When sharing the survey results with practitioners and highlighting that process mapping seemed to be so widely adopted as a core activity, CI practitioners were unsurprised by this result. The propensity for selecting process mapping as a core CI activity appeared to be driven by the level of understanding of CI held by the decision makers responsible for the CI implementation. One practitioner shared this perspective:

> *Not all of the leaders have a strong background in continuous improvement. … process mapping seems to be this go-to tool because it is graphical…can be easily understood by most audiences in leadership.*

In some instances, process mapping itself had become the 'improvement' as it was often seen as a proxy for improvement. Customer outcomes at times were a second-order consideration to the capturing

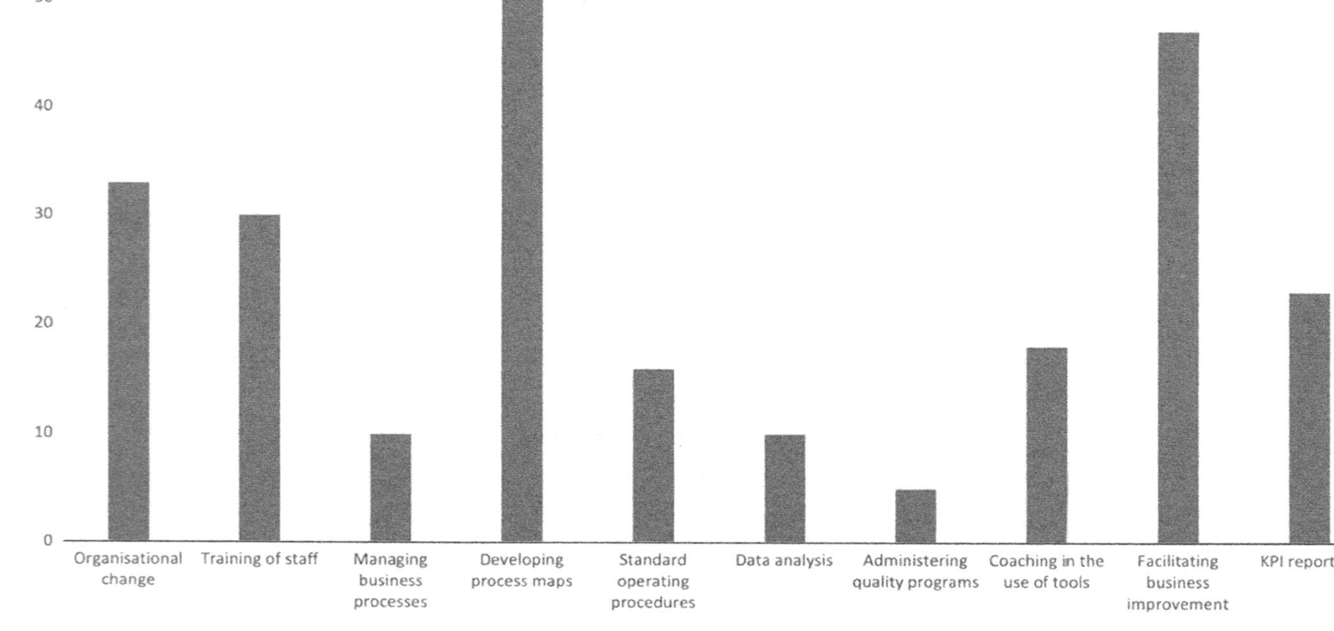

Figure 7.2 Practitioner core activities.

of the activities. This was outlined in the statement by another CI practitioner:

> *My GM has KPIs on every single team that have to do three process maps a quarter, but there's no KPIs around actually improving anything or the customer's outcome in the end.*

Putting the documentation of processes (i.e. process maps/procedures) at the centre of what constitutes an improvement outcome may unintentionally emphasise the tool at the expense of the intended purpose of CI. Making tangible and measurable improvements centred on an understanding of process and the customer is a core tenet of CI, one which may be lost when the focus is predominantly on the application of a tool instead.

In contrast to the proportion of CI practitioners who engaged in process documentation as a core activity, almost half as many CI practitioners reported engaging in performance measurement and data analysis as a core activity of CI work. Similar, to the application of process mapping, developing measures without a focused on process and the customer also has some unintended consequences. This was highlighted in the following comments by a CI practitioner involved in the development of performance measures:

> ...just some performance measures [that] no one really kind of understood... where they had come from...they didn't really have much in the way of, I guess, substance in terms of what it meant to people. People were just reporting on stuff.

Limiting the investment of CI practitioner time on working with teams to develop '*internal capability*' for measurement may result not only in a lack of understanding regarding how to measure performance but also whether process improvements result in outcome improvements. This can have a further negative impact on the perceived value of CI. Consequently, this may hinder the embedding of CI as an organisational practice beyond achieving process improvements of 'low-hanging fruits' projects (Radnor & Johnston, 2013 p. 905), or being perceived as the next fad of management.

This is not to say that the local government sector does not use performance measurement. In fact, the respective state governments in Australia and at the federal level in New Zealand, drive various top-down KPI regimes which local government organisations are required to report their performance against (Johnsson, Pepper, Price &

Richardson, 2021). However, what seems to have emerged from our engagement with CI practitioners in both countries is a perceived lack of integration between the high-level KPI reporting requirements and the translation of these into operational performance measures that are actionable and that can be used alongside CI interventions to achieve performance improvements. This was highlighted in the following statement from a CI practitioner:

> *They give us all the data and everything, but it's not meaningful data. We're not tracking meaningful things and reporting on... or doing anything with the information that we're collecting. We're not using the data to inform our decision-making about the services that we're delivering and how well we're doing and all of that sort of stuff. We're really just collecting figures that don't mean anything and putting them in the reporting process.*

Taking such an approach to measurement as part of a CI initiative is likely to make quantifying and demonstrating the impact of improvement projects difficult. This in turn may further impact the level of engagement, management commitment and long-term viability of such projects.

Working more strategically

Results from the survey also showed that 33% of CI practitioners reported engaging in change management activities. The importance of strategic work such as this as part of CI initiatives should not be underestimated. Change management work facilitates the positioning of CI as a key organisational values and practice as part of strategic development. In instances where this was occurring, CI practitioners reported positive results. In discussing how they were working at a strategic level, many practitioners reported focusing on articulating the value that CI can bring to the organisation's strategic planning. The following insight from a practitioner who participated in our research summed up the broader experiences of working towards embedding CI at a more strategic level:

> *...just starting to really embed...one of our values was continuous improvement, and our vision included the word excellence, and everybody was aware of our vision and values, how they connected into our strategic planning.*

Taking a strategic approach and embedding CI values were also initiated at an operational level. At this level, CI was embedded as part of the processes for the development and implementation of business planning. This also enabled the business plans to address improvements that that directly linked to community priorities. CI reinforced the link between the operational business planning process and the community strategic planning framework. A CI practitioner responsible for the application of the community strategic planning framework (which in the Australian state of New South Wales is a mandatory requirement for all councils) talked about this relationship:

> *I think once we start showing the executive team…the improvements that we're making, then there'll be even more of an appetite for it across the business…[we are working to] change how we develop our business plans, as well as how the operational plan … meaningful targets and track our results better, and then make informed decisions that's going to be the place that we start.*

As we discussed in Chapter 2 as a key feature of the evolving nature of CI practice in local government, Service Delivery Reviews (also referred to a service review) emerged as a key approach. CI practitioners adopted Service Delivery Reviews were used as a way of deploying CI more strategically by considering broader organisational impacts both internally and with respect to customers. The framework adopted by the CI practitioners in our research draws on the work of the Australian Centre for Excellence in Local Government. In the 'how to' manual (Hunting, Ryan & Robinson, 2014 p. i), a service delivery review aims to:

> *'Drive more efficient use of resources whilst providing services to meet the needs of the community. In the context of this manual, a service delivery review can take a 'whole of organisation' approach or just cover one department, service or strategic focus area'*

From our interviews with practitioners implementing service delivery reviews, we uncovered that the framework was adopted in various ways. In some instances, the CI practitioner took a leadership role in conducting the service delivery review. In other instances, CI practitioners supported service managers and teams in leading a review of their own services. When working with managers and their teams, support was not only during the review phase but also continued through the implementation of the resulting organisational changes which stemmed from the review. For example:

> ...So along with the service reviews, we're actually supporting implementation... so I've got a staff member currently working with our BA team implementing, doing changes for them, leading their team for them and making a difference...the accountability for the implementation of a review falls squarely with the manager and director of the service that has been reviewed...in terms of the programs' success, that accountability falls I guess with me...

Within the application of service delivery reviews, there appeared to be three central foci—cost, legislative requirements and customer needs. This is highlighted in the following comment from a CI practitioner who had been adopting this framework for some time in their organisation:

> ...Yeah, look, most of the service reviews that we have done over the years, certainly cost has been a very strong focus. As mentioned before legislative compliance is always very high on the priorities, and also applying the customer to that as well, and really having that strong understanding.

This is not surprising given the contextual characteristics of local government which include a state-driven legislative framework, finite resource availability and a growing focus on understanding and translating the diverse community needs into 'customer value' propositions.

Other practitioners reported having initiated the application of service delivery reviews prior to implementing the community strategic planning framework. However, we found that service delivery reviews were sometimes conducted in isolation, similar to the application of process mapping discussed above. When service reviews were implemented without a link to the overall strategic direction, these were not universally perceived to be the most beneficial in achieving alignment with broader community outcomes. This is highlighted in the following comment from a CI practitioner involved in this work:

> ...[as part of] the continuous improvement program...when we first started [there] was going to be rolling program of service reviews. We've identified that that's not where the most benefit will be for the organization in the next two years. For us, it's

around getting the foundations right…[we]...It will be doing things around developing that four-year plan, essentially, and saying, "Here's what the next four years looks like. Here is what the costings are going to be" …let's take a longer term view and have a look at those sort of external factors that are happening in a growth context that are likely to have impacts on your resourcing requirements.

What appears to have emerged from our work with CI practitioners is the need to ensure that Service Delivery Reviews are firmly grounded in the strategic direction of the organisation and their application is contextualised and deployed in ways consistent with organisation capabilities at a particular point in time. The fit between service delivery reviews and other management practices is essential for their ongoing deployment and relevance as an organisational practice. Furthermore, the acceptance of service changes that such reviews recommend is also contingent on such fit.

Use of consultants

A finding that emerged from our focus groups with CI practitioners was the degree to which consultants were used in CI work. The use of consultants was common. Consultants were used in a number of different ways, including: provision of training in CI tools and frameworks; organisational self-assessments (using the ABEF criteria); process reviews; process mapping and project planning. Often working as independent providers (rather than from larger consultancy firms), the consultants were often professionals who had either previous local or State government experience or had held CI roles in the private sector.

In some organisations, the use of consultants was strategic, embedded in the broader CI program and designed to develop organisational capability and broader engagement with CI. The comment below highlights this approach:

…whenever we have used consultants, we've very much taken the approach that they're not people just to come in, do something and walk out… we've always made sure that it's well connected with our strategic direction, that any delivery of any information from a consultant is done in a partnering way with a permanent member of staff, so that we can actually continue to share that learning. I guess the consultants that we have used in the past have been used to

> *almost up skill us as Continuous Improvement Practitioners within the organization.*

The use of consultants seemed to bring the most value when the organisation recognised that the role of consultants was to embed capabilities and competencies not already in the organisation. An effective approach discussed by the CI practitioners in our research was engaging with the consultant to develop training tools and resources that could then be contextualised and deployed by the organisational CI practitioners themselves. This helped to build a sense of ownership, as highlighted in the following comment:

> *We certainly had that leadership throughout that service review process from [consultant], and [consultant] assisted us in developing our training materials so that it was actually delivered by us for us.*

In other instances, the work of consultants did not seem to be connected to the broader strategic direction. In such instances, it was not sufficiently resourced or contextualised. This had an impact on the potential benefits that could be achieved from engaging with external expertise. This is highlighted in the following comment:

> *... apparently there was a review of finance and a review of the admin area...the administration and customer service area is quite complex, [yet] someone came in for two days and did a desktop analysis and left a list...that's not helpful [and] apparently the same was done in finance...I think that if you want step change, and you want behavioural change, and a shift in culture, you need to have someone with skin in the game.*

Though the use of consultants as discussed above can be beneficial when deployed as part of a broader organisational strategy, internal ownership and responsibility of a CI program cannot be outsourced. It was recognised that developing CI organisational competence, trust and internal relationships was necessary. Engaging directly with CI work persistently over a period of time was a way in which some organisations created sustainability in this work. This is reinforced in the comment below.

> *So I'm just very cognizant of the people aspect of continuous improvement and I don't think that you can be truly successful,*

> *and embed real and sustainable continuous improvement and change unless you have got willing participants that are actually going to do the [work]. And that takes time, and that can be really frustrating for people, and consultants come in, they're not going to build those relationships with people.*

What is demonstrated from the experiences that were shared with us is there are benefits to be gained by drawing from external expertise to build organisational capability. This is most beneficial when consultants are part of a broader strategy and framework for CI. Commitment and ownership must be intrinsic to the organisation. This was particularly important when undertaking reviews of processes that require substantial organisational changes to be made.

Concluding comments

A number of learnings have emerged from our work with CI practitioners. There are two levels at which CI work is practiced: operational and strategic. Operational and strategic work was not talked about as being mutually exclusive. Rather, different practitioners working in different contexts have talked about how they have invested more or less time and resources focusing more on one level. There seemed to be a tendency to start CI work at the operational level, with significant time working on processes mapping. For some practitioners, process mapping was used to lay the foundational understandings of CI in the organisation. Interestingly, moving beyond process mapping was recognised as difficult by many practitioners and only a few were able to secure executive support to work at a more strategic level. One way in which work at the strategic level was achieved was by adapting CI and linking CI directly to State policy imperatives, such as the Integrated Planning and Reporting Framework (NSW) and the Service Delivery Review framework (across Australia). Yet, when it came to performance measurement, CI practitioners recognised that there were not making strong links between this aspect of CI and State-driven policy imperatives on performance measurement and reporting.

When we invited CI practitioners to discuss barriers to the implementation of their CI programs at a strategic level, participants consistently reported that management buy-in, organisational culture, time and resourcing to do improvement projects and level of expertise in quality in the organisation were barriers that challenged them. These aspects represent the elements of change management. We maintain that change management and how to implement change across the organisation is a key area for development to support CI practitioners—particularly focusing on the important relationship between people and processes.

One way in which resourcing and a limited level of expertise (particularly with change management) were addressed was through the use of consultants. This was a common practice, adopted by all participants in our research. However, the way in which consultants were engaged differed across organisations. Those CI practitioners that reported positive outcomes from working with consultants emphasised the importance of maintaining internal ownership and the responsibility for doing improvement work by managers and their teams. This close engagement with the improvement work facilitated the sharing of knowledge by consultants in ways in which build organisational capability and longer-term sustainability of CI. This aspect is particularly important to sustain organisational changes made as a result of investment in consultancy services and support.

References

Hunting, S.A., Ryan, R. and Robinson, T.P. 2014. *Service delivery review: A how to manual for local government, Australian Centre of Excellence for Local Government* (2nd ed.), University of Technology, Sydney.

Johnsson, M.C., Pepper, M., Price, O.M. and Richardson, L.P. 2021. "Measuring up": A systematic literature review of performance measurement in Australia and New Zealand local government. *Qualitative Research in Accounting & Management*, 18(2), pp. 195–227. https://doi.org/10.1108/QRAM-11-2020-0184.

Radnor, Z. and Johnston, R. 2013. Lean in UK Government: Internal efficiency or customer service? *Production Planning & Control*, *24*(10–11), pp. 903–915. https://doi.org/10.1080/09537287.2012.666899

8 Conclusion

Key insights from the book

We began with this book by considering the complexity of local government. Local government exists and operates in an environment characterised by various political machinations imposed and enacted by multiple levels of Government. These machinations influence the local government priorities, policies, funding, parameters of performance and what constitutes good governance. In addition to the political complexities inherent in the governance of these organisation, they must also articulate and deliver value to numerous and diverse stakeholder groups in an efficient and effective manner. In attempting to navigate and respond to internal and external complexity, local government organisations have adopted various Quality and CI frameworks and approaches.

The adoption of various Quality and CI frameworks and approaches has evolved over several decades in response to changing contextual conditions (e.g., New Public Management, Best Value, Fit for the Future). A way in which CI has been sustained by some organisations has been to find ways to use CI which are responsive to top-down state governments' policies, changing priorities and stakeholder needs. One way in which such responses have been articulated and persued in practice is to connect CI to existing ways of working. These have included: adopting CI approaches and methodologies deemed to be successful in other local government organisations; harnessing already existing competencies and skills and attempting to adapt CI by investing in the contextualisation of frameworks; embedding CI as part of the everyday ways of doing work and producing hybridised approaches that work in-situ.

The literature and case studies suggest that those local government organisations, which have made inroads to adapting, adopting, or

DOI: 10.4324/9781003011675-8

embedding CI were able to maintain focus on finding ways of meeting the emerging needs of internal and external stakeholders. In contrast, those organisations that have been less successful at contextualising CI have tended to experience resistance towards such initiatives. This resistance has, in general terms, occurred because Quality or CI has been perceived as just another program or fad imposed by management with limited resourcing. This has had a significant impact on the buy-in to Quality or CI throughout the organisation.

Continuous improvement must begin with a willingness and commitment to invest in contextualisation. This requires challenging not only how things are done and how services are designed, delivered, measured, and improved, but also the very frameworks and approaches of CI that are put to use. As with any change journey, the embedding of a chosen CI framework takes time and persistence even when results are not immediately visible. One strategy that is often used in the early stages of program implementation is to focus on 'low-hanging fruit' (Radnor & Osborne, 2013 p. 275) such as the implementation of tools (e.g. process mapping) to demonstrate the potential power of Quality and CI. Though useful as a means of introducing such programs, our case research and the literature discussed suggest that in many instances Quality and CI programs do not move beyond these initial pilot programs. The risk with focusing only on a 'low hanging fruit' strategy is, of course, that beyond proof of concept for the CI program, it may quickly realise diminishing returns. This is because there are only limited 'low hanging fruit' projects to be targeted within any one organisation. The sustainability of continuous improvement over the long term relies on the considered development, embedding and ongoing refinement as part of everyday work and practice.

The importance of learning and knowledge sharing cannot be underestimated in embedding sustainable improvement in local government. Well-established Quality and CI philosophies (such as Kaizen) remind us of the importance of learning and knowledge sharing as both a driver and outcome of CI. When considering the implementation of CI as an organisational program, we propose in this book that the use of the Organisational Knowledge Creation Theory (OKCT) and knowledge sharing framework (Nonaka 1991; Nonaka and Toyama, 2003) may facilitate the embedding of sustainable CI in organisations. This research-informed framework may be used by practitioners to support 'workers' experiences, learnings, and acquired knowledge are inherited accumulatively and shared' (Nakamori et al., 2019 p. 273). Sharing of experiences and bits of knowledge may then be harnessed to inform improvement in organisational structures, systems and ways of working.

The case studies discussed in part two of this book have focused on stakeholder analysis, performance measurement and management, critical success factors, the work of CI practitioners. Future case study research in this field is particularly important to bringing theoretical and practice work together. This provides an opportunity for closer alignment between the work of practitioners and academics in ways that may support knowledge sharing and deeper insights to be discovered. Such collaborations and mutual contributions may strengthen the development of new understandings informing theory development and evidence-based practice. These present several key take-aways which we further discuss in the following paragraphs.

As discussed above, a key element of the complex environment in which local government organisations operate are stakeholders. Therefore, it is essential for local governments to understand, manage, and respond to multiple and diverse stakeholders and their needs which may present conflicting objectives. For CI practitioners, the importance of stakeholders in the success of CI projects cannot be underestimated. The book offers CI practitioners a proposed 10 step process for analysing and managing stakeholders and their needs. This process can be used to enable CI leaders and those involved in CI projects to understand, negotiate, and manage multiple interests associated with a CI project. Like any tool, this must of course be contextualised to both the organisation and the project and other management and CI practices.

Though part of the local government discourse for some time now, performance measurement and management still appear to be an area of work that CI practitioners find challenging and that managers have reported as being a complex undertaking. Our case research and in the literature, challenges with the implementation of performance measurement and management suggests that this may be due to several factors that may be at play. These include: (1) a lack of investment in the development of performance measurement and management capability; (2) breadth of strategic and policy priorities (often driven by the State) and (3) the complexity of local government operations. In this book, we have offered a framework and a process to support practitioners in the development of performance measurement and management systems for their organisations. The framework links strategic priorities and outcomes with operational performance measures. It also recognises that strategic and operational measurement is an iterative process that requires refinement in response to the changing priorities and needs of stakeholders. As the framework brings to the fore operational measurement, it sheds light on the relationship between key processes and core activities and thus may support the identification of improvement initiatives that support functional and strategic integration.

As we acknowledge the complexities involved in implementing CI in local government, it is important for CI practitioners to understand some of the critical factors required for the successful implementation of CI projects. Based on our research, we have identified ten critical success factors in the Australia-New Zealand context. These are: top management commitment, middle management support and involvement, project champion, commitment to the indigenous community, speed of project planning and execution, effective communication, organisational culture, project selection, adequate resources, and inclusive stakeholder management. While some of these factors (e.g. top management commitment) have been already identified in earlier research, some new critical success factors (e.g. commitment to the indigenous community) have been included in our study that focussed on the Australia New Zealand context.

In implementing Quality and CI programs, local government organisations tend to invest in workforce resources through the employment of CI practitioners as well as engaging consultants. In undertaking their work, CI practitioners engage work in two distinct, but related ways. When working operationally, CI practitioners tend to focus on deploying tools such as process mapping as a way of introducing CI in the organisation. However, several practitioners reported that when adopting more analytical approaches to CI, including process measurement, some difficulties were encountered. These difficulties are encountered because such organisation-wide initiatives such as performance measurement and data-driven CI require greater investment in capability development which cannot always be supported due to resource constraints. Those CI practitioners who were successful in extending CI work at a more strategic level and thus were able to adapt and embed CI within industry-based frameworks such as the Integrated Planning and Reporting Framework (NSW) and the Service Delivery Review Framework (across Australia). This enabled them to leverage existing and additional resources by demonstrating the ongoing relevance of Quality and CI in also facilitating the implementation of frameworks newly introduced by the respective State Governments.

Whether working at an operational or strategic level, CI practitioners recognised that their success in embedding CI was contingent on management and organisational commitment. The investment in time and resourcing to do improvement projects and bolster organisational expertise in Quality and CI often occurs through the use of consultants. This was found to be a common practice adopted by the local government. CI practitioners reported that the way in which they engaged with consultants, had an impact on the degree to which CI capability and knowledge were harnessed and embedded in the organisation.

Several ideas have emerged from work in this book for future research endeavours. Firstly, performance measurement and management would benefit from further research inquiry. As discussed in detail in already published work by the authors of this book (see for example Johnsson, et al., 2021), key areas for consideration for further research includes work focused on:

- Stakeholder or 'citizen-centric measures' and how these may be interrelated with already existing operational efficiency and effectiveness measures.
- Understanding the historical and policy drivers which have shaped (and some would argue even appropriated) the discourses of performance management and measurement in local government.
- Case studies that help to uncover the development of performance measurement and management systems sensitive to specific local government contexts (e.g. urban, peri-urban, country contexts).
- Case studies that situate performance measurement in Quality and CI initiatives.

A second area of focus for future research draws on the need for further and more recent case studies regarding the application of various CI models in local government. Specifically, how such models are contextualised and interlinked with other emerging local government initiatives such as service delivery reviews, industry benchmarking, integrated planning and so on. In fact, there is a clear opportunity for more scholarly research on these local government initiatives themselves in the A&NZ context and how these may be associated with improved community outcomes.

The third area pertains to extending understandings of the practices of knowledge sharing and how these may (or not) be enacted in local government organisations. Consideration may be given to the kinds of bits of knowledge share and how this sharing might take place. Another area for further research may focus on discovering the kinds of conditions that facilitate or hinder sharing of knowledge as an organisational practice in the local government context. CI-focused research may look towards understanding how knowledge sharing may be harnessed to facilitate improvement initiatives.

Finally, we proposed further research be conducted to investigate the work of Quality and CI practitioners. Specifically, we proposed a research focus on the work and practices of CI practitioners in the local government setting. Questions could be structured around the investigation of the different levels at which CI practitioners deploy CI and how they may be more or less able to influence strategic change. Further inquiry could consider the kinds of competencies that are necessary for CI practitioners to have the greatest impact in embedding Quality and CI in A & NZ local government organisations.

References

Johnsson, M.C., Pepper, M., Price, O.M. and Richardson, L.P. 2021. "Measuring up": A systematic literature review of performance measurement in Australia and New Zealand local government. *Qualitative Research in Accounting & Management*, *18*(2), pp. 195–227. https://doi.org/10.1108/QRAM-11-2020-0184

Nakamori, T., Takahashi, K., Han, B.T. and McIver, D. 2019. Understanding KAIZEN practice in Japanese overseas manufacturing: a framework. *International Journal of Knowledge Management Studies*, *10*(3), pp. 271–298.

Nonaka, I. 1991. The knowledge-creating company. *Harvard Business Review*, *69*(6), pp. 96–104.

Nonaka, I. and Toyama, R. 2003. The knowledge-creating theory revisited: knowledge creation as a synthesizing process. *Knowledge Management Research & Practice*, *1*, pp. 2–10. doi.org/10.1057/palgrave.kmrp.8500001

Radnor, Z. and Osborne, S.P. 2013. Lean: A failed theory for public services? *Public Management Review*, *15*(2), pp. 265–287. https://doi.org/10.1080/14719037.2012.748820

Appendix

Chapter 2 Useful readings and resources

The following sources which include readings and publicly accessible websites are useful to provide a deep dive into specific topics introduced in this book.

Dollery, B.E., Kortt, M.A. and Grant, B., 2013. *Funding the future: Financial sustainability and infrastructure finance in Australian local government*. Federation Press.

Musli, M, Mann, R, Grigg, N and Wagner, JP, 2011, Business Excellence Model: An overarching framework for managing and aligning multiple organisational improvement initiatives, Total Quality Management & Business Excellence, 22:11, 1213–1236, DOI: 10.1080/14783363.2011.624774.

Megarrity, L, 2011, Local government and the Commonwealth: an evolving relationship Research Paper no. 10 2010–11. Accessed 22/3/21 https://www.aph.gov.au/About_Parliament/Parliamentary_Departments/Parliamentary_Library/pubs/rp/rp1011/11RP10#_Toc284229058.

Radnor, Z., Osborne, S.P., Kinder, T. and Mutton, J., 2014. Operationalizing co-production in public services delivery: The contribution of service blueprinting. *Public Management Review*, Vol. 16 No. 3, pp. 402–423.

Sanchez, L and Blanco, B, 2014, Three decades of continuous improvement, Total Quality Management & Business Excellence, Vol. 25 no. 9–10, pp. 986–1001.

Sreedharan, V.R. and Raju, R., 2016. A systematic literature review of Lean Six Sigma in different industries. *International Journal of Lean Six Sigma*. Vol. 6 no. 6, pp. 430–466.

Australian Centre of Excellence for Local Government (ACELG)

https://www.uts.edu.au/research-and-teaching/our-research/institute-public-policy-and-governance/about-institute/centre-for-local-government.

Accessed 1/09/20.

CouncilMark™ https://councilmark.co.nz/ Accessed 10/01/21.

LGAM, 2020 Australian Business Excellence Framework http://www.lgam.info/australian-business-excellence-framework) Accessed 1/09/20.

New Zealand Business Excellence Foundation. https://nzbef.org.nz/ Accessed 1/09/20.

SAI Global Australian Business Excellence Framework, 2015. https://www.saiglobal.com/improve/excellencemodels/businessexcellenceframework/. Accessed 1/09/20.

Chapter 4 Questionnaire for conducting a stakeholder analysis

The following questions help to gather information about stakeholders to commence the stakeholder analysis process.

1. Who are the main individuals and groups who can influence the success of your council's continuous improvement project?
2. Why are these individuals and groups interested in your council's continuous improvement project?
3. What are the processes used by your local council to communicate and consult the stakeholders? Are these processes efficient?
4. How effective are the transactions and negotiations between your council and your stakeholders?
5. Which of your stakeholders are supportive, opposed, or neutral to your continuous improvement project?
6. Which stakeholders of your continuous improvement project are powerful? Does any of them fail to conduct themselves in socially acceptable behaviour? Which stakeholders have to be dealt with urgently?
7. Overall, how would you rate your council's ability to manage the stakeholders? High? Medium? Low?

Template: Stakeholder acceptance table

The following template may be used to categorise stakeholders as supportive, neutral and opposed.

Stakeholders (insert stakeholder name)	*Supportive*	*Neutral*	*Opposed*

Key:
+ +: Highly supportive
+: Supportive
0: Neutral
−: Opposed
−−: Highly opposed

Chapter 5 Performance measurement resources

This appendix outlines a summary of the methodology adopted to implement the PMM framework and *Municipal* Council.

Methodology stages

The methodology for the development of the PMM consisted of seven stages. These are shown in the figure below and discussed in detail in the following sub-sections.

1 Project scoping

Project scoping is the first step of the process and it requires collaboration among the organisation key personnel and project leaders. In this initial phase, it is important to:

- Articulate project aims, objectives and outcomes;
- agree on the overall scope of the project (and consider examples of what might be out of scope);
- agreement on what key outputs may look like;

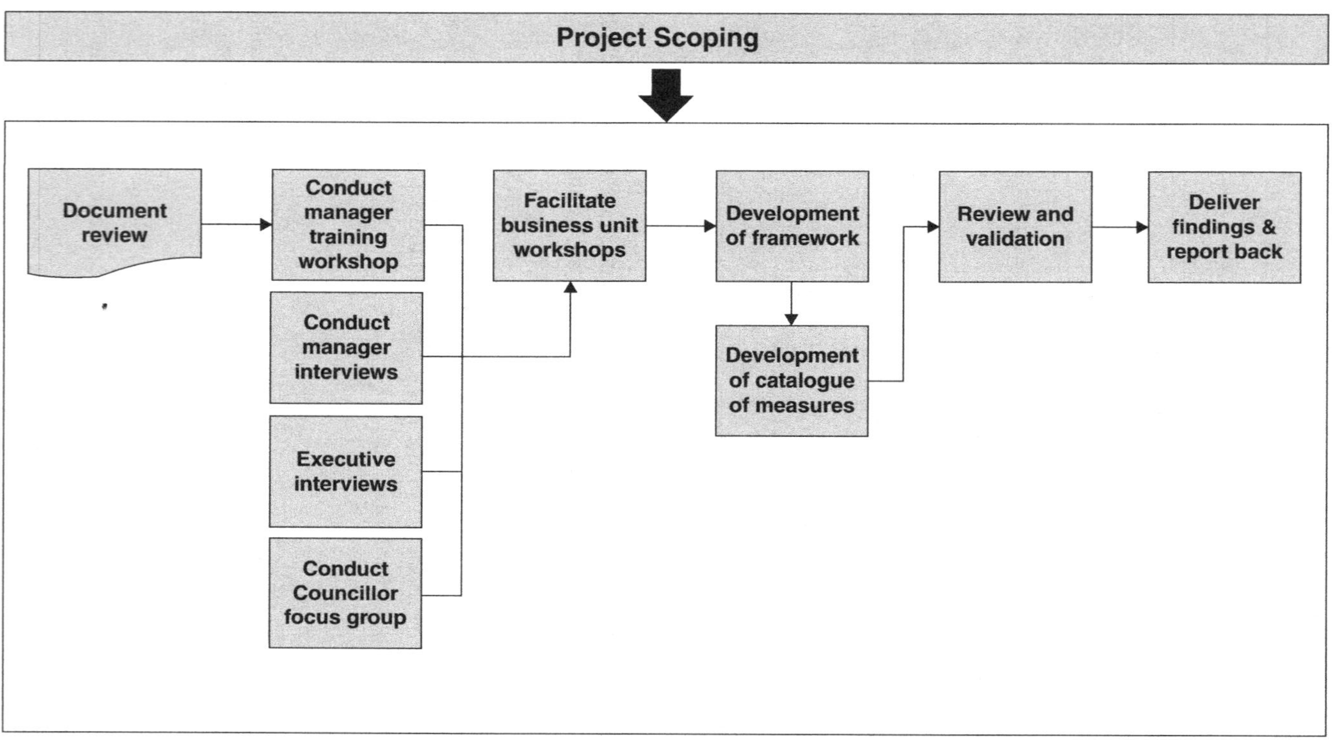
Project Scoping
Document review
Conduct manager training workshop
Conduct manager interviews
Executive interviews
Conduct Councillor focus group
Facilitate business unit workshops
Development of framework
Development of catalogue of measures
Review and validation
Deliver findings & report back

- agree on key personnel and their roles and responsibilities;
- develops the project plan outlining key milestones (ensuring the incorporation of key organisational events, e.g. planning, budgeting and reporting cycles; local government elections);
- agree on progress reporting and communication strategies.

In the case of the development of the PMM framework discussed in Chapter 5, these discussions took place between the Executive team, project sponsor (a member of the executive), organisational project manager and the project leads (the authors of this book).

2 Document analysis

Analysis of organisational documents is essential for orienting the project team to the nature of the organisation and its approaches to PMM.

In the case of the project outlined in Chapter 5, over 20 organisational documents were reviewed as a precursor to interviews with business managers, executives and Councillors. The kinds of documents that were reviewed included:

- *Planning documents and reports*
- *Resourcing strategy documents*
- *Operational plans*
- *State Government documents, framing planning and performance measurement*
- *Existing organisational performance measures*

3 Interviews, focus groups and manager's workshop

Interviewing managers and team leaders and conducting focus groups with the elected Council provide insights into:

- Scope of work of each business unit;
- existing measurement practices;

- challenges faced by managers and executives in developing performance measurement;
- challenges faced by managers and executives reporting against existing performance measures;
- elected council expectations about performance reporting.

Furthermore, insights from these kinds of activities can be used to ascertain organisational understandings about performance measurement and management and to frame insights about competency levels in this domain of work. This level of engagement helps to articulate the learning needs of managers and their direct reports, informing the learning objectives and design of the managers' workshop.

> *In the case of the project outlined in Chapter 5, the learning objectives*
>
> *The objectives of the workshop state were as follows:*
>
> 1. *Work together to develop our understanding of the relationship between function, plans and services*
> 2. *Define, map and articulate measures a service for each unit*
> 3. *Link selected service to CSP & Delivery Plan*
> 4. *Plan the next step to articulate the performance measurement and management framework*

4 Facilitate unit workshops

The purpose of the facilitated unit workshops with managers and team leaders is to introduce measurement concepts and make explicit the relationship between measurement and operational activities. These concepts can then be applied to the development of unit and team measures.

> *In the case of the project outlined in Chapter 5, the objectives of these workshops include:*
>
> - *Introduce measurement concepts*
> - *Document core work activities*
> - *Link operational measures to core activities.*

- *Document outcome measures to reflect business unit foci.*

Participants were asked to consider the following questions to articulate the work of their business unit:

- *What work does your business unit do for the council?*
- *What are the services that your business unit provides?*
- *What are the key activities of your business unit (team)?*
- *What constitutes customer satisfaction?*
- *Tell me more about ... (relationships that exist internally/externally)*
- *How do you know when the activities of your unit have achieved the desired outputs/outcomes?*
- *What measure would demonstrate such outputs/outcomes?*

Once key areas of work were identified and agreed upon, discussion about how to measure performance commenced. Participants were asked to consider the following questions

- *Of the measures currently reported, which relate to the processes and activities discussed?*
- *Which of the processes and activities that you have outlined are/are not currently measured?*
- *What do you currently report on and does it reflect the processes and activities discussed?*

Responses to the above question were captured and documented by the research team. Examples of how the core activities and measures were captured during workshops.

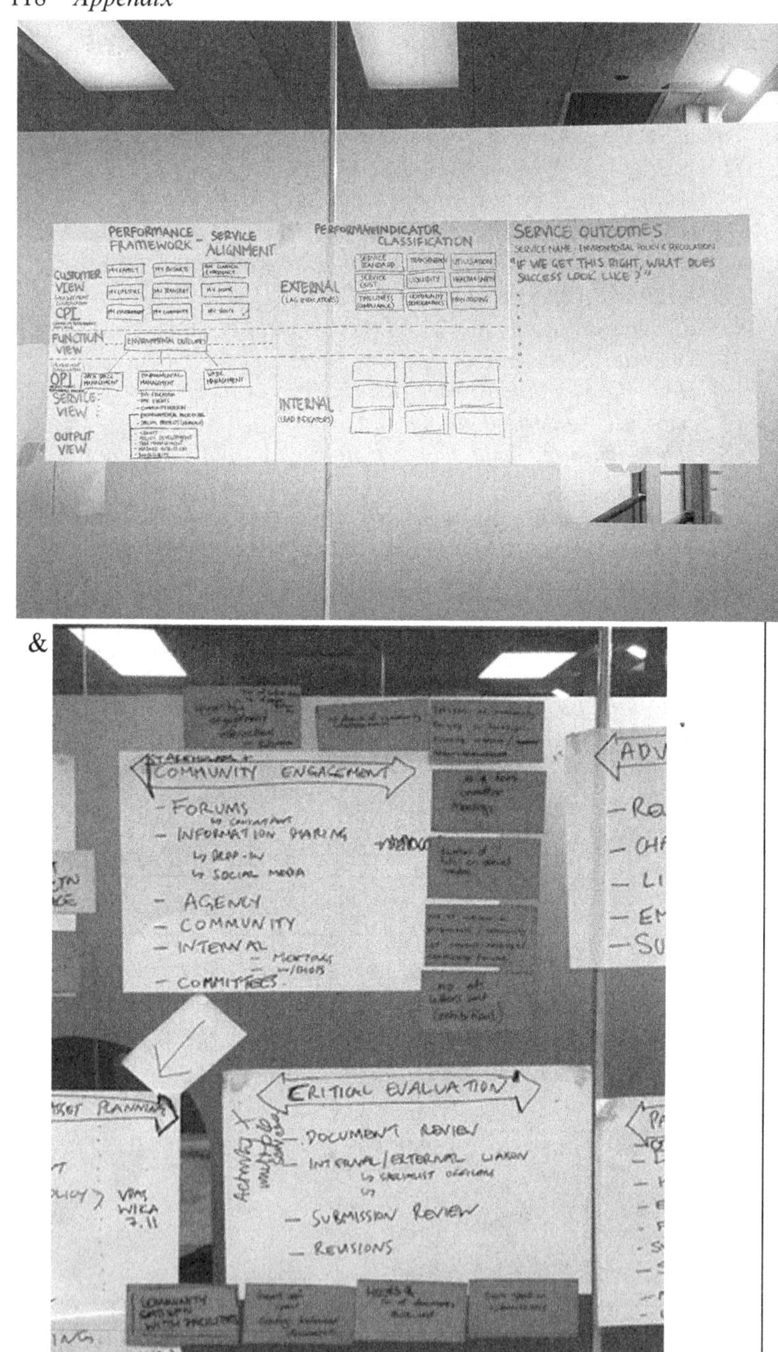
PERFORMANCE FRAMEWORK - SERVICE ALIGNMENT
PERFORMANCE INDICATOR CLASSIFICATION
SERVICE OUTCOMES
"IF WE GET THIS RIGHT, WHAT DOES SUCCESS LOOK LIKE?"
CUSTOMER VIEW
CPI
FUNCTION VIEW
OPI
SERVICE VIEW
OUTPUT VIEW
EXTERNAL
(LAG INDICATORS)
INTERNAL
(LEAD INDICATORS)
COMMUNITY ENGAGEMENT
- FORUMS
- INFORMATION SHARING
- SOCIAL MEDIA
- AGENCY
- COMMUNITY
- INTERNAL
- COMMITTEES
CRITICAL EVALUATION
- DOCUMENT REVIEW
- INTERNAL/EXTERNAL LIAISON
- SUBMISSION REVIEW
- REVISIONS

&

5 Development of framework and measures catalogue

A performance measurement framework needs to show the integration between strategic outcomes and operational performance measures. Therefore, the framework needs to:

- Interconnect different layers of measurement operational lead and lag measures and strategic outcome indicators;
- illustrated the relationship between key processes core activities and measures.

The case of the project outlined in Chapter 5, the structure of the framework is shown below:

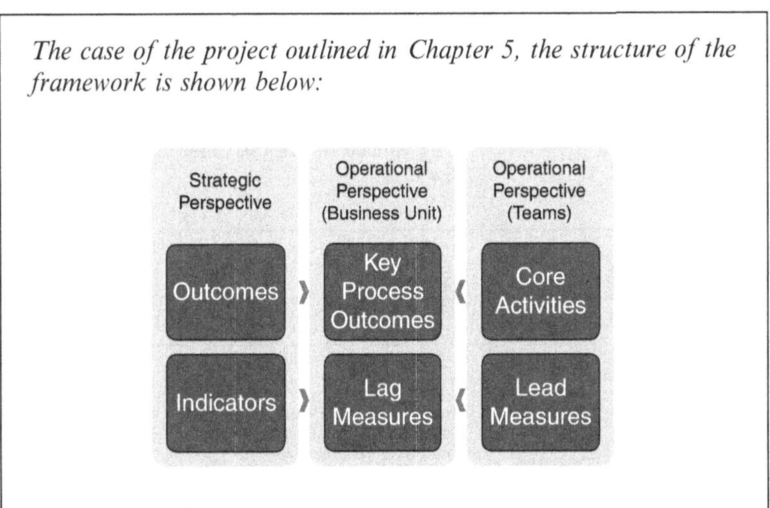

The measurement catalogue is based on the PMM framework. The purpose of the catalogue is to collate key processes, activities and measures into a single source document. A measurement catalogue needs to be flexible enough for:

- Inclusion of multiple levels of measurement;
- future iterations of measures to be included;
- integration of new core services and associated operations;
- obsolescence of existing core services and associated operations.

In the case of the project outlined in Chapter 5, the measurement catalogue included various levels of measurement as shown below:

Strategic Area of focus	**Outcome indicator**
Customer	Overall satisfaction
Customer	Satisfaction with facilities
People	Employee satisfaction
People	Turnover rate
Resourcing	Operating performance ratio
Resourcing	Own source revenue ratio
Infrastructure	Network average pavement condition
Infrastructure	Average cost of road maintenance per km
Service	Embed service outcomes once developed
Service	Embed service outcomes once developed

Business Unit	**Key Process**	**Activities**	**Lead Measure**	**Calculation**	**Unit of Measure**	**Frequency**	**Manager Responsible**
Compliance	Environment & Health	Inspections, Investigations, Approvals, Enforcements	Cooling tower Inspections	Cooling tower Inspections/ Total Number	Percentage	Quarterly	Manager Compliance Team Leaders
Compliance	Environment & Health	Inspections, Investigations, Approvals, Enforcements	Skin penetration premises	Skin penetration premises/ Total Number	Percentage	Quarterly	Manager Compliance Team Leaders
Compliance	Environment & Health	Inspections, Investigations, Approvals, Enforcements	UPS tank inspections	UPS tank inspections/ Total Number	Percentage	Quarterly	Manager Compliance Team Leaders

6 Review and validation

The review and validation phase is important because it allows for managers and team leaders to reflect on the work completed. In particular, it allows the utility of the identified measures to be considered, as well as the capacity to populate such measures with appropriate data. The outcome of this phase is to have the performance measurement catalogue confirmed, in anticipation of data collection and reporting. This phase may have a number of iterations allowing managers and team leaders to rationalise and refine the final set.

In the case of the project outlined in Chapter 5, the process of review and validation of measures was deployed with the following steps:

- *Review identified measures*
- *Clarify measures definitions and associated frequency of reporting*
- *Confirm which of the identified measures are currently being reported*
- *Determine which of the identified measures will require new data collection mechanisms to be established*
- *Identify any gaps in the identified measures*
- *Articulate any additional measures*

7 Reporting back

In the final project phase, it is important to provide feedback to project sponsors and executives. This may take the form of a final report, including recommendations for embedding the new PMM Framework and associate catalogue. Furthermore, presentations and Q&A sessions may be helpful to clarify those recommendations and future actions.

Glossary of terms for measurement work

Goal: An observable and measurable end result or outcome. Sometimes goals are broken down into one or more objectives to be achieved within a more or less fixed timeframe.

Objective: More specific and easier to measure ends result. A number of objectives might all contribute to a broader organisational goal.

Strategy: The actions taken to achieve a set goal. Goals should be specific enough to be measurable via lag/outcome and lead/driver measures

Measure: A number or quantity that records a directly observable value or performance. All measures have a unit attached to them, e.g. dollar, litre, kilograms; volume etc.

Lag/Outcome measure: Measures whether the goal has been achieved.

Lead/Driver measure: Measures whether you are on track to achieve the goal.

Target: The magnitude (relative size) of what is being measured

Lead (Driver) and lag (Outcome) measures: Help highlight the cause and effect relationships between goals and objectives.

Key Performance Indicator: Describe a service factor quantity used as a representation (i.e. de-facto measure) of an associated (but non-measured or non-measurable) factor or quantity

Lead indicators (or performance drivers): May comprise multiple measures that inform the future state.

Lag indicators (or performance outcomes): May comprise multiple measures tell you what has happened.

Chapter 6 Critical success factors checklist

In initiating a CI program, the following checklist may facilitate the identification of areas that need to be supported through focused investment and resources to maximise the success of the program.

Critical success factor	*Questions*	*Yes/ No*	*Action points*
1. Top management commitment	Have we obtained a commitment from the Chief Executive and other members of the council leadership team?		

(*Continued*)

Critical success factor	*Questions*	*Yes/ No*	*Action points*
2. Middle management support & involvement	Have we discussed the scope of the project with middle managers? Are they supportive? Are they actively involved (for projects already started)?		
3. Project champion	Is there a champion in this project? If not, have we identified a project champion?		
4. Commitment to the indigenous community	Have we designed an appropriate process to engage with the main indigenous community in your area?		
5. Speed of project planning and execution	Is the project planning/project execution too fast?		
6. Effective communication	Does this project have effective communication with its different stakeholders?		
7. Organisational culture	Is the organisational culture conducive for this continuous improvement project?		
8. Project selection	Is this the right project that should be implemented at this point of time?		
9. Adequate resources	Have we allocated a budget for this project? Are the right people involved in this project? Have we done workload planning for this project?		
10. Inclusive stakeholder management	Have we identified all stakeholders of this project? Are the stakeholder engagement processes efficient? Are the stakeholder negotiations effective?		

Index

Printed in the United States
by Baker & Taylor Publisher Services